Five Teaching and Learning Myths—Debunked

Drawing from research in developmental and educational psychology, cognitive science, and the learning sciences, *Five Teaching and Learning Myths—Debunked* addresses some of the most commonly misunderstood educational and cognitive concerns in teaching and learning. Multitasking, problem solving, attention, testing, and learning styles are all integral to student achievement but, in practice, are often muddled by pervasive myths. In a straightforward, easily digestible format, this book unpacks the evidence for or against each myth, explains the issues concisely and with credible evidence, and provides busy K–12 teachers with actionable strategies for their classrooms and lesson plans.

Adam M. Brown and **Althea Need Kaminske** are Founding Co-Directors of the Center for Attention, Learning, and Memory at St. Bonaventure University, USA.

Other Eye On Education Books Available from Routledge (www.routledge.com/eyeoneducation)

Coding as a Playground:
Programming and Computational Thinking in the Early Childhood Classroom
Marina Umaschi Bers

The Bridge to School:
Aligning Teaching with Development for Ages Four to Six
Claire Bainer, Liisa Hale, and Gail Myers

Teaching Children with Challenging Behaviors:
Practical Strategies for Early Childhood Educators
Edited by Gayle Mindes

Anti-Bias Education in the Early Childhood Classroom:
Hand in Hand, Step by Step
Katie Kissinger

Nurturing Young Thinkers Across the Standards:
K–2
Wynne A. Shilling and Sydney L. Schwartz

Developing Natural Curiosity through Project-Based Learning:
Five Strategies for the PreK–3 Classroom
Dayna Laur and Jill Ackers

The Self-Regulated Learning Guide:
Teaching Students to Think in the Language of Strategies
Timothy J. Cleary

Sticky Assessment:
Classroom Strategies to Amplify Student Learning
Laura Greenstein

Eco-Education for Young Children:
Revolutionary Ways to Teach and Learn Environmental Sciences
Ann Lewin-Benham

Five Teaching and Learning Myths—Debunked
A Guide for Teachers

Adam M. Brown
and Althea Need Kaminske

NEW YORK AND LONDON

First published 2018
by Routledge
711 Third Avenue, New York, NY 10017

and by Routledge
2 Park Square, Milton Park, Abingdon, Oxon, OX14 4RN

Routledge is an imprint of the Taylor & Francis Group, an informa business

© 2018 Taylor & Francis

The right of Adam M. Brown and Althea Need Kaminske to be identified as authors of this work has been asserted by them in accordance with sections 77 and 78 of the Copyright, Designs and Patents Act 1988.

All rights reserved. No part of this book may be reprinted or reproduced or utilised in any form or by any electronic, mechanical, or other means, now known or hereafter invented, including photocopying and recording, or in any information storage or retrieval system, without permission in writing from the publishers.

Trademark notice: Product or corporate names may be trademarks or registered trademarks, and are used only for identification and explanation without intent to infringe.

Library of Congress Cataloging-in-Publication Data

A catalog record for this book has been requested

ISBN: 978-1-138-55665-2 (hbk)
ISBN: 978-1-138-55667-6 (pbk)
ISBN: 978-1-315-15023-9 (ebk)

Typeset in Utopia
by Apex CoVantage, LLC

Contents • • • • •

Meet the Authors *vii*
Acknowledgements *ix*

Introduction *xi*

1 Multitasking *1*

The Myths *1*
The Research *2*
  Myth 1: Multitasking allows your brain to work on several projects at once *2*
  Myth 2: Multitasking is a useful skill that allows people to accomplish several tasks simultaneously in an efficient way, saving time and increasing productivity *5*
  Myth 3: Multitasking helps you deal with distractions (prevents procrastination) *7*
  Myth 4: Through practice, children, adolescents, and adults get better at multitasking *7*
The Tools *9*

2 Examples *13*

The Myths *13*
The Research *13*
  Myth 1: Using an example helps students generalize *15*
  Myth 2: Examples make the topic interesting *17*
  Myth 3: Making the material relatable or interesting automatically leads to learning *18*
The Tools *20*

3 Focus *27*

The Myths *27*
The Research *27*
  Myth 1: The ability to focus is inborn: some people have it, some people don't *28*

Myth 2: The best way to improve focus on real-world tasks is to avoid distractions by finding a quiet area with nothing to distract you   29
Myth 3: I can still focus, even with my cell phone   30
Myth 4: Getting distracted and letting your mind wander isn't a big deal   31
The Tools   33

4   Testing   37

The Myths   37
The Research   37
   Myth 1: Testing only rewards test-taking skills and doesn't actually help students learn   40
   Myth 2: Testing promotes teaching to the test   43
   Myth 3: Testing doesn't measure learning   43
   Myth 4: There are two types of students: bad test takers and good test takers   44
   Myth 5: Testing causes undue anxiety and distress that is harmful to students   45
The Tools   46

5   Learning Styles   53

The Myths   53
The Research   53
   Myth 1: Every person has their own learning style, some are visual learners, some are kinesthetic, some linguistic, etc.   55
   Myth 2: Teaching in the student's preferred learning style makes a difference in how well the student will learn the information   56
   Myth 3: It is good practice to identify students' learning styles and create lesson plans to address those learning styles   59
   Myth 4: There is no danger in teaching to students' preferred learning styles   60
The Tools   61

Afterword: Technology in the Classroom   65
Glossary   71

Meet the Authors

Adam M. Brown received his Ph.D. in Educational Psychology and Statistics and his Certificate of Advanced Study in Educational Research from the State University at Albany, SUNY. He is an Associate Professor in the School of Education at St. Bonaventure University, where he serves as founding co-director of the Center for Attention, Learning, and Memory with his co-author. His research interests include attention and learning, teratogens, and development. In his free time he jumps on the trampoline with his daughter Annabelle, spends time in his wood shop, works on his family's bison ranch, and enjoys time with loved ones.

Althea Need Kaminske received her Ph.D. in Cognitive Psychology from Purdue University. She is an Assistant Professor in the Psychology Department at St. Bonaventure University and founding co-director of the Center for Attention, Learning, and Memory. She has won numerous teaching awards and studies student learning, metacognition, and cognitive processes. In her spare time, she plays board games, goes on hikes with her dogs, and is a valuable member of her kickball team.

Acknowledgements

It is entirely unfair that the cover only displays the authors' names. Many people contributed to the final version of this book. We have been very fortunate to have colleagues, students, and friends provide crucial content and invaluable edits to this volume, and we owe them a great debt.

First, we would like to thank our graduate research assistants for the tireless hours of diligent work. We want you to know that we value your time and effort. Well done James Bates, Joseph Hayes, Martha Zimmerman, Michael Healy, and Katelynn Brown.

Second, we would like to thank those with keen eyes for editing. Substantial changes were made in light of your insight and reflection: James Bates, Nancy Casey, Lisa Eppolito, Rene Hauser, Pauline Hoffman, Craig Sinesiou, and Karen Bauernschmidt.

We cannot thank you enough for your contributions. Your feedback made us rethink our manuscript, making it more understandable, coherent, and readable. Your enthusiasm and insightful comments improved the quality of this text.

—Adam & Althea

Introduction

How Do We Learn?

This is a simple question with a complicated answer. This question is hard to answer because it is so close to us. Our learning, our memory, and our thinking are very intimate parts of our inner lives. Sometimes our memory fails us at embarrassing moments or our attention wavers despite our best efforts. We see others succeeding where we have failed and maybe have even been pleasantly surprised when we have done well where others have not. Being so close to this process of learning makes it difficult to view learning objectively. It's tempting to think that what may work for others doesn't work for us because we are the exception to the rule. This is because learning doesn't always feel like an objective, step-by-step process when we are the ones learning. When it's going well, learning feels transformative, enlightening, and maybe even thrilling. And when it's not going well, learning feels frustrating, difficult, and maybe even humiliating. Learning feels deeply personal and individual because it is happening to us.

> Basic research on human learning and memory, especially research on human metacognition ... has demonstrated that our intuitions and beliefs about how we learn are often wrong in serious ways. We do not ... gain an understanding of the complexities of human learning and memory from the trials and errors of everyday living and learning. ... [P]eople hold beliefs about how they learn that are faulty ... which frequently leads people to ... teach in nonoptimal ways.
> (Pashler, McDaniel, Rohrer, & Bjork, 2008, p. 117 (1))

This dichotomy in learning experiences—from the transformative to the frustrating—has led to no shortage of theorizing, discussion, and research. There is a sea of theories and ideologies around education and learning. Some are useful, evidence-based theories with tried and true practices to back them up. Others are persistent myths based on messy interpretations and clever branding. Fortunately, educators and researchers have devoted their careers to better understanding learning and how it can be improved. The purpose of this book is to help you evaluate some of the most common myths surrounding attention, memory, and learning.

In each chapter of this book we will introduce a myth about teaching and learning and break it down into its associated myths. For example, in the first chapter, "Multitasking," we first address the myth that multitasking is actually *being able to do multiple tasks at the same time*. Then we address associated myths: "Multitasking is a useful skill" and "Multitasking makes you more productive." After introducing the myth we will give an overview of the research surrounding that myth and how the evidence-based principles apply to each of the associated myths in the *Research* section. Finally, at the end of each chapter in the *Tools* section, we will give some suggestions on how to apply these evidence-based principles in the classroom: from early elementary classrooms to high school and college classrooms. These developmentally appropriate pedagogical tools are designed to be flexible and modifiable. For example, we list high school and college classroom tools together for both developmental reasons and for practical reasons. All the tools selected for the high school classroom can be easily modified and applied to college classrooms. The *Tools* sections are meant to serve as helpful examples and are by no means an exhaustive list of ways to incorporate the research that is covered in each chapter. Rather, they serve as models to demonstrate practical ways to use these concepts on a day-to-day basis.

Chapter 1: "Multitasking" will evaluate the myth that we can successfully work on multiple tasks at the same time. In the *Research* section we will review new research that shows that multitasking actually hurts our learning far more than it helps. Finally, in the *Tools* section we will give some ideas for how to avoid inadvertently making students multitask and how students can avoid common temptations to multitask.

Chapter 2: "Examples" will explore the myth that an example can improve learning by making the topic more interesting or relatable. In the *Research* section we will review research on examples, problem solving, and interest that shows how examples can distract from and confuse the lesson at hand. In the *Tools* section we will give tips and examples for how to use examples to engage and inform students.

Chapter 3: "Focus" will evaluate the myth that focus is an inborn trait—something that some people have and some people don't. The *Research* section will look at the surprising research on how we can actually improve our focus by adding distractions as well as new research on how cell phones destroy our focus. In the *Tools* section we will give some activities that will help build students' focus.

Chapter 4: "Testing" will explore the myth that testing is harmful to learning. We will look at the research demonstrating that testing, as retrieval practice, can be a powerful learning tool as well as some of the issues surrounding the design of tests. In the *Tools* section we will give examples of activities that use retrieval practice to improve learning without grading students.

Chapter 5: "Learning Styles" will examine the myth that students learn best when instruction is tailored to a specific modality (i.e. visual, verbal, kinesthetic, etc.). In the *Research* section we review how all learners can benefit from multiple modes of instruction using dual coding. In the *Tools* section we will give some ideas on how to use dual coding to reinforce learning for all students.

In all the chapters we have used *Connections* boxes to let our readers know how each of our chapters is conceptually related to concepts in other chapters. We have done this to demonstrate both the interrelatedness of the chapters, but also for our readers to begin to see the bigger picture for our classrooms.

In all the chapters we have also included a *Development* box that explores research with children and young students. Here we address research that speaks to the developmental changes that occur as we grow and learn.

At the end of each chapter is a helpful *Summary* box that bullets the most important concepts, condensing them for our readers so nothing is overlooked or forgotten.

To conclude, in the Afterword: Technology in the Classroom we discuss how each of the myths contributes to the use and misuse of technology in the classroom.

Finally, at the end of the book we include a Glossary. Glossary terms are in bold throughout the book.

We know you love to learn. We know you want to learn more about factors that help and harm learning. We know this because you took the initiative to read this book and your initiative is admirable.

This book has been designed specifically for our colleagues in classrooms: teachers, professors, and teacher educators. It is a guide for those who have a love of learning and want to know more about cutting-edge information on how learning occurs. We have deliberately used language to make this information accessible to a wide population. This book is an attempt to bring research on attention, learning, and memory to those who can best implement changes to classrooms, programs, districts, universities, and legislation. Unlike most books you have read, the discussion need not end with this book. We are available to answer questions or concerns; please contact us at the Center for Attention, Learning, and Memory, sbucalm.blog. We hope you enjoy this book.

● ● ● ● ●

Reference

1. Pashler H, McDaniel MA, Roher D, Bjork RA (2008) Learning styles: Concepts and evidence. *Psychological Science in the Public Interest* 9(3):105–119.

1

Multitasking

Originally the term **multitasking** was a computer term referring to a computer's ability to run multiple programs or tasks simultaneously. Gradually this term came to be used to refer to some people's ability, or skill, to get many things done seemingly simultaneously. In today's world we refer to multitasking as a much desired skill, suggesting that some people possess this skill and others do not. How wonderful to be able to work on several projects at once, read several documents at a time, do homework while watching television, take notes on your laptop while jumping back and forth to Facebook, and all the while getting notifications from your phone about incoming texts, tweets, Instagrams, and calls.

Research reveals that multitasking negatively affects memory. This is true even if the tasks are simple. Contrary to what you might think, digital natives (students who grew up in the digital age and who are used to frequent digital media) perform no better at instructional multitasking than do those who are naïve to the digital world (1). Another important point to consider is that habitual media multitasking increases "mind wandering," decreasing attention to relevant tasks. Students who multitask make significantly more errors because the brain has difficulty trying to attend to both tasks simultaneously (or rapidly switch from one to the other).

The Myths
1. Multitasking allows your brain to work on several projects at once.
2. Multitasking is a useful skill that allows people to accomplish several tasks simultaneously in an efficient way, saving time and increasing productivity.
3. Multitasking helps you deal with distractions and prevents procrastination.
4. Through practice, children, adolescents, and adults get better at multitasking.

The Research

Research on multitasking from neuroscience, cognitive psychology, and educational psychology reveals that multitasking is actually **attention switching**. In other words, when we are engaged in what we feel is multitasking, we are really just rapidly switching our focus from one task to another. Rapid attention switching results in poor attention and poor cognitive performance, while simultaneously reinforcing the task switcher for task switching (2). Furthermore, even though an experienced task switcher may be well practiced at task switching, their cognitive performance remains low (3). Switching attentional focus takes time and wastes resources. Not only does switching attention increase total amount of time on task, but each time we switch our focus, our brain engages in a multiple step process. Each time you switch between tasks your brain has to:

1. Stop the current task.
2. Search for information about the new task.
3. Find new task parameters.
4. Engage in the new task.

These steps take time and attention, even if it feels like it happens automatically. This is where we waste time, make more mistakes, and impair our deep thinking. Worse than that, repeatedly engaging in attention switching harms our ability to stay on topic by ignoring distractions. Rather than maintaining focus, our brains expect, and seek distractions because they have been trained to switch (see Chapter 3: Focus). When we avoid deep thinking by task switching our memory and learning are harmed (4).

> To make matters worse, lots of multitasking requires decision-making. Decision-making is also very hard on your neural resources and ... little decisions appear to take up as much energy as big ones. One of the first things we lose is impulse control. This rapidly spirals into a depleted state in which, after making lots of insignificant decisions, we can end up making truly bad decisions about something important. *Why would anyone want to add to their daily weight of information processing by trying to multitask?*
> (Levitin, 2014, p. 98, emphasis added (5))

1. Myth: Multitasking allows your brain to work on several projects at once

> **RESEARCH: Rather than working on several tasks simultaneously, our brains have limited attentional resources (we have trouble thinking about more than one task at a time).**

Perhaps the biggest myth about multitasking is that it allows us to work on several tasks at the same time, when in fact we are switching rapidly between many tasks. Multitasking always comes with an **attentional switch** cost. For example, in an article from *Frontiers in Human Neuroscience*, researchers asked participants to decide whether sentences were plausible or not (e.g. "This morning I ate a bowl of cereal" vs. "This morning I ate a bowl of shoes") in a variety of attention conditions. Participants did best in **single tasking** conditions, conditions where participants were performing only one task. Participants also did well in the **selective attention** conditions, i.e. where they had both visual and auditory distractors but were told to ignore these distracting stimuli. Participants in the multitasking condition did the worst and made significantly more errors than participants in the other conditions (6).

Importantly, there are two stages that reliably contribute to the attentional switch cost of attempting to multitask: task-preparation and selective attention (7). Specifically, when students are given time to prepare, the cost of task switching goes down and when students' ability to focus and ignore irrelevant information is better, the cost of task switching goes down. The longer students are given between tasks the less of a performance cost. With a longer time between one task and the next task, student performance increases and task switch costs decrease. However, it is important to understand that task-preparation helps any task, not just when switching tasks.

Monsell (8) reports, in an article on task switching found in the journal *Trends in Cognitive Sciences*, that individual responses are significantly slower and tend to have more errors directly after a task switching. The author's review article investigated the fine tuning of task switching and found that a task switch can cause problems for a number of reasons. First, there is a switch cost in time between different tasks to get readjusted to the new task. And second, a preparation effect. The preparation effect can be reduced if you know a task is coming. According to Levitin (5) "Because attention switching is metabolically costly, it's good neural hygiene for your brain to give it time to switch into the mindset of your next task gradually and in a relaxed way before the next task is begun" (p. 320).

When people engage in task switching it not only hurts their attention and performance on the task, it also hurts their memory. For example, research recently published in the journal *Memory* reported on a study that investigated the impact of memory for faces. Wammes and Fernandes (9) found that "the largest declines in memory performance occurred when the concurrent tasks (multitasking) required the same processing resources, and also used the same material set as that in the target recognition task" (p. 198). They demonstrated that when participants were multitasking there was a 42 percent decline in recognition memory for faces. This outcome is explained by a competition between task-relevant and task-irrelevant information. It was also found that multitasking negatively affected both short-term and long-term memory. Bottom line, it was more difficult for participants to remember if they had seen a face if they had been multitasking at the time they saw the face.

Multitasking hurts both memory for facts and memory for how-to-do something. Research published in 2016 in the journal *Memory & Cognition* investigated declarative (facts) and procedural (how-to) memory through the introduction and use of novel tools. Memory for what the tools looked like and what they could do was lower for those who were multitasking in comparison with the performance of those who were single tasking. This tells us that declarative memory, or memory for facts, is harmed during multitasking. Further, when multitasking, procedural (how-to-do) memory is also harmed. People showed low levels of accuracy both for how to use the tools and for demonstrating how to hold the tools in the multitasking condition (10).

The availability of media in our everyday lives makes it easier to multitask than ever. **Media multitasking** is using multiple forms of media simultaneously while performing several tasks. An example would be a student studying, with FaceBook open, a favorite TV show playing, and the phone chirping away as texts, tweets, and other notifications come in. Media multitasking negatively affects student performance (11). When students use multimedia during a lecture their learning is impaired compared to students who take notes with traditional pencil and paper. According to Wood, Zivcakova, Gentile, Archer, De Pasquale, and Noska (11) "contrary to popular beliefs, attempting to attend to lectures and engage digital technologies for off task activities can have a detrimental impact on learning" (p. 365). Not only does media multitasking hurt memory and learning, the more we engage in media multitasking, the more it hurts us. People who tend to multitask with many forms of media have poorer memory for information they had seen in the past (12). Researchers found that those people who use more media multitasking have a "wider attentional scope" which means they pay attention to more task-irrelevant information, hurting their ability to pay attention to task-relevant information because there is a competition for space.

Media multitasking becomes more harmful the more we engage in it because it essentially teaches us to become distracted more easily (3). Loh, Tan, and Lim (4) investigated distractibility of media multitasking using several different groups: 1) an undistracted (single-tasking) group, 2) a distracted group, and last, 3) a multitasking group. The undistracted group test scores averaged around 93 percent correct. In the distracted group average scores dipped a bit, hovering about 89 percent correct. Most important is that the scores of the multitasking group who were listening and reading (similar to being in a typical class where a Power Point presentation is being given) were significantly lower, averaging about 74 percent correct. What's just as interesting is participants who reported that they spent much of their day-to-day life multitasking scored worst and reported that they had to exert more effort to complete the task. The researchers reported that "extensive daily media multitasking directly reinforces task switching behavior and deteriorates the ability to sustain attention on a focal task" (p. 120). Essentially what this research reveals is that 1) reducing multitasking reduces distractibility, increasing test scores and 2) habitual media multitasking increases "mind wandering," decreasing attention to relevant tasks.

Connections

In an interesting 2016 study titled "Attention and the testing effect," researchers found that retrieval practice was more effective in the multitasking condition (13). What this means is that one of the few interventions that does impact and help decrease the negative effects of multitasking is quizzing. See Chapter 4 on Testing for more on retrieval practice.

---

2. Myth: Multitasking is a useful skill that allows people to accomplish several tasks simultaneously in an efficient way, saving time and increasing productivity

> **RESEARCH: Multitasking should be avoided because rather than saving time, it costs time, and decreases productivity.**

Multitasking hurts our ability to accomplish tasks in several ways. Even simple tasks can hurt your ability to keep information in short-term memory. Likewise, simple tasks can interfere with recalling information, if those tasks divert attention. What tasks can divert attention? Any task that requires thinking can divert attention away from other information you are trying to memorize or learn. Further, the more time spent on the task, the longer attention is diverted. Multitasking is inefficient because you aren't really doing multiple tasks at once; you're switching between multiple tasks and there are costs to those switches. More than a decade ago it was reported in the *Journal of Experimental Psychology* (14) that "switching between two cognitive tasks results in large and reliable increases in reaction time and error rate" (p. 228). More recently, researchers have found that any interruption or task switching hurts performance (15, 16). What's more, while task switching impairs memory for whatever is being attended to, data indicate that task switching improves memory for irrelevant things. So, what this means is that when people attempt to multitask they add information to their memory that isn't relevant to either task while simultaneously reducing their memory of either task being attended to (1)!

Multitasking is less productive even if the task does not require much thinking time, in other words: simple tasks. Furthermore, contrary to popular belief, digital natives perform no better at multitasking than those who are naïve to the digital world (17). Worse, memory for a task or event is especially compromised when a person is operating (or feels like they are operating) under a time constraint (14).

Multitasking is unproductive both because of the increased errors people make when attempting to multitask and because of how much longer people take to complete tasks while attempting to multitask (8, 14). For example, Rubinstein, Meyer, and Evans (18) report that as the complexity of the task increases, the time it takes to switch back and forth increases. The same thing goes for familiarity, if the task or subject is new to you, task-switching time increases. The reason for this is that our brains run on a rule activation system. This system activates rules used for a task, then when we switch attention, the system must shift gears to a different set of rules. The less familiar you are with those rules, or the more complex the rules are, the longer it will take your brain to activate the rule set and re-engage with the task.

Although multitasking harms our ability to accomplish thinking tasks, there is emotional gratification (feeling entertained or relaxed) that promotes the behavior. The association of a good emotional feeling with an undesirable task makes the task seem "not so bad." This association then leads to the thinking task becoming more desirable, and the multitasking behavior is then repeated, which ultimately reinforces the cycle. An example of this is watching TV and doing homework: the TV impairs the cognitive aspect of the homework, but makes it feel more entertaining, which promotes the repetition of multitasking behavior (2).

Connections

Our ability to perform a task can be especially impaired if the tasks or stimuli are similar or related. In those cases, we can intertwine information from the separate tasks in long-term memory rather than separating them, causing increased task switch costs. Ultimately what this

> means is that students are better off studying one subject for a while, taking a small break to avoid task-switching pitfalls, and then studying a totally different subject for a while. Repeating this cycle helps learning and memory for several of the reasons outlined above. This very important point is relevant for classroom planning and especially important for studying. For more on this process, referred to as *interleaving*, see Chapter 4: Testing.

3. Myth: Multitasking helps you deal with distractions (prevents procrastination)

> **RESEARCH:** *Rather than helping you deal with distractions, multitasking promotes both distraction and procrastination.*

Not only does multitasking harm your attention, learning, and memory, it trains you to be distracted easily. We talked about this with media multitasking in the first multitasking myth, however, it's important to note that this is true of all multitasking, not just when it happens with media. A relevant research article by Wendt, Kiesel, Mathew, Luna-Rodriquez, and Jacobsen (19) asked people to complete tasks in the presence of distractions. They found that distractions harm the productivity of completing the tasks. This is not so surprising. Whether single tasking or multitasking the distractions have a negative effect on productivity. However, the effect was greater for those that were multitasking. This informs us of a few things as educators. Decreasing distractions in general helps productivity. Furthermore, if we are attempting to multitask, then distractions amplify the task-switching cost.

4. Myth: Through practice, children, adolescents, and adults get better at multitasking

> **RESEARCH:** *Study after study shows us that repeatedly engaging in multitasking does not increase our ability to make it more productive. Instead, it worsens the problem because we are training our brain to "want" to switch (increasing distractibility).*

Unfortunately, many students multitask while studying. An article in the journal *Computers in Human Behavior* reports on the use of social media and texting while studying. Results show that students who use social media score significantly lower on tests and those who text and use social media while studying have lower GPAs. Further, students were only able to stay on task for six minutes before switching tasks (20).

Students need to be more aware of time management and how to maintain attention while studying. As Levitin (5) puts it, "Organizing our mental resources efficiently means providing slots in our schedules where we can maintain an attentional set for an extended period. This allows us to get more done and finish up with more energy" (p. 176).

In the article "Corresponding influences of top-down control on task switching and long-term memory," the authors report that when individuals attempt to multitask they remember fewer words that they were trying to commit to memory and more words that were irrelevant to the task. In other words, when you try to multitask you will accidentally learn a bunch of things you didn't plan to at the expense of learning what you intended to (1).

Development

Attention switching and selective attention (see Chapter 3: Focus) are separate but related processes. Attention switching "is a separate ability which has to develop to overcome the stickiness of selective attention" (21, p. 624). As children develop (age 3 to 6) they become better at switching attention to different tasks.

Researchers investigating attention in child development reveal that children attempting to multitask are rapidly switching attention, just like adults (22). As reported in *Cognitive Brain Research*, fMRI suggests that task switching is controlled for by many brain regions. The same regions that are associated with task switching also are associated with task repetition, indicating that task switching may not be a strength of the human brain (23).

Performance for all ages increases on tasks where attention is on one channel. However, attention shifting is even more difficult for younger children. Compared to adolescents and adults, younger children see more disruptive effects in learning (22). Worse, according to research from *Language and Cognition*, task switching decreases attentional focus on the task while simultaneously increasing distractibility (24)! This article tells us that not only is it harder for young children to mentally switch tasks, it also makes them more distractible.

Summary

- Multitasking does not allow you to complete multiple tasks simultaneously, instead when you think you are multitasking you are actually switching between tasks.

- This task switching comes at a cost, including making more errors and increasing reaction time. This cost is amplified if the tasks are complex or unfamiliar.
- Task preparation reduces the cost of task switching.
- Task switching hurts memory for facts, how-to-do memory, images, and faces, while simultaneously increasing memory for irrelevant information.
- Off-task media multitasking harms learning (examples here are cell phones and computers in class).
- Even simple tasks can force task switching, making memory and learning suffer.
- Distractions hurt memory, no surprise here. However, distractions hurt even more if one is multitasking.
- Children are especially bad at multitasking and by practicing multitasking they paradoxically increase distractibility and mind wandering.

●●●●●

The Tools

Multitasking always leads to a decrease in performance—students make more errors, remember less, and take longer to complete activities. Avoid situations in the classroom that encourage attention switching (multitasking). For example, having students write down notes from a presentation while simultaneously listening to a lecture forces attention switching.

Early Elementary

- **Check-Ins:** Ask important and relevant questions about the material. These should not be trick questions. These are simply an attention check. If the student is paying attention to the lesson and relevant material these should not come as surprises or difficult to answer questions.
- **In Your Own Words:** During individual or group work sessions, ask the student to explain why they are doing what they are doing. Ask them to explain in their own words why they have decided to approach the problem the way they have.
- **Brain Break:** During the instruction period, allow for structured pauses in the presentation of material. This provides the students with an opportunity to get up, stretch out, or simply break from

constantly focusing on material. This technique has been shown to prolong students' ability to focus over longer periods of time.
- **Break Tasks into Pieces:** This method of instruction allows the students to have material geared toward his or her individual needs. Throughout an assignment or lesson, have the student focus to complete a part of the task, then take a break, and come back to finish the task. This method increases productivity of the student by allowing the student to focus on a small portion of the assignment at a given time.

Late Elementary

- **Content Check:** At the end of lessons, routinely conduct Content Checks with students. The instructor will randomly distribute cards numbered 1 through 4 to the students. Each of the number cards will relate to a question or idea presented on the board. 1. What are we doing? 2. Why are we doing it? 3. How did you determine what you were doing? 4. What is your next step? The students will answer these questions in their small groups to reinforce the lesson and determine what methods they are using.
- **Teacher-Centered Direct Instruction:** This method of instruction requires that students focus their attention on the presenter and the material that is relevant to the topic. If students do not focus their attention they will misunderstand material. This is a more straightforward approach to commanding focus and attention.

Middle School

- **Buzz Session:** While in small groups, instructors will give students content-specific problems to solve in short time periods. The students in the group will work together and the instructor will monitor student progress. Once the question is answered, the students will report their findings and explain how they came to their conclusion.
- **Modeling:** This technique works by providing students with a visual of what it is that they are to do. Having a visual representation of the steps involved in completing a task allows for students to focus on the relevant tools and information for effectively completing a task.

High School and College

- **Think, Pair, Share:** The think, pair, share method of instruction provides the students with appropriate time to evaluate the material provided. Instructors will lecture or provide information to the students for 15–20 minutes, then allow students two to three opportunities within the lecture period to answer questions or discuss material in groups. This activity allows students to evaluate material from the lesson and demonstrate to the instructor what information they have gained and where the students are still struggling.

● ● ● ● ●

References

1. Richter FR & Yeung N (2015) Corresponding influences of top-down control on task switching and long-term memory. *The Quarterly Journal of Experimental Psychology* 68(6):1124–1147.
2. Wang Z & Tchernev JM (2012) The "myth" of media multitasking: Reciprocal dynamics of media multitasking, personal needs, and gratifications. *Journal of Communication* 62:493–513.
3. Ophir E, Nass C, & D. WA (2009) Cognitive control in media multitaskers. *PNAS* 106(37):15583–15587.
4. Loh KK, Tan BZH, & Lim SWH (2016) Media multitasking predicts video-recorded lecture performance through mind wandering tendencies. *Computers in Human Behavior* 63:943–947.
5. Levitin DJ (2014) *The organized mind: Thinking straight in the age of information overload* (Dutton, New York, NY).
6. Moisala M, Salmela V, Salo E, *et al.* (2015) Brain activity during divided and selective attention to auditory and visual sentence comprehension tasks. *Frontiers in Human Neuroscience* 19:1–15.
7. Vandierendonck A, Liefooghe B, & Verbruggen F (2010) Task switching: Interplay of reconfiguration and interference control. *Psychological Bulletin* 136(4):601–626.
8. Monsell S (2003) Task switching. *Trends in Cognitive Sciences* 7(3):134–140.
9. Wammes JD & Fernandes MA (2016) Interfering with memory for faces: The cost of doing two things at once. *Memory* 24(2):184–203.
10. Roy S & Park NW (2016) Effects of dividing attention on memory for declarative and procedural aspects of tool use. *Memory & Cognition* 44:727–739.
11. Wood E, Zivcakova L, Gentile P, *et al.* (2011) Examining the impact of off-task multi-tasking with technology on real-time classroom learning. *Computers & Education* 58:365–374.
12. Uncapher MR, Thieu MK, & Wagner AD (2016) Media multitasking and memory: Differences in working memory and long-term memory. *Psychonomics Bulletin and Review* 23:483–490.
13. Mulligan NW & Picklesimer M (2016) Attention and the testing effect. *Journal of Experimental Psychology: Learning, Memory, Cognition* 42(2):938–950.
14. Rodgers RD & Monsell S (1995) Costs of a predictable switch between simple cognitive tasks. *Journal of Experimental Psychology: General* 124(2):207–231.
15. Lepine R, Bernardin S, & Barrouillet P (2005) Attention switching and working memory spans. *European Journal of Cognitive Psychology* 17(3):329–345.
16. Kiesel A, Steinhauser M, Wendt M, *et al.* (2010) Control and interference in task switching: A review. *Psychological Bulletin* 5:849–872.

17. Dindar M & Akbulut Y (2016) Effects of multitasking on retention and topic interest. *Learning and Instruction* 41:94–105.
18. Rubinstein JS, Myer DE, & Evans JE (2001) Executive control of cognitive processes in task switching. *Journal of Experimental Psychology: Human Perception and Human Performance* 27(4):763–797.
19. Wendt M, Kiesel A, Mathew H, Luna-Rodriquez A, & Jacobsen T (2013) Irrelevant stimulus processing when switching between tasks. *Zeitschrift fur Psychologie* 221(1):41–50.
20. Rosen L, Carrier LM, & Cheever LA (2013) Facebook and texting made me do it: Media-induced task-switching while studying. *Computers in Human Behavior* 29:948–958.
21. Hanania R & Smith LB (2010) Selective attention and attention switching: Toward a unified developmental approach. *Developmental Science* 13(4):622–635.
22. Gomes H, Molholm S, Christodoulou C, Ritter W, & Cowan N (2000) The development of auditory attention in children. *Frontiers in Bioscience* 5:108–120.
23. Dove A, Pollman S, Schubert T, Wiggins CJ, & Yves von Cramon D (2000) Prefrontal cortex activation in task switching: an event-related fMRI study. *Cognitive Brain Research* 9:103–109.
24. Brito NH, Murphy ER, Vaidya C, & Barr R (2015) Do bilingual advantages in attentional control influence memory encoding during a divided attention task? *Bilingualism: Language and Cognition* 19(3):621–629.

2

Examples

As much as educators want to improve performance in the classroom, we ultimately hope that students are able to use the skills they learn in class in their everyday lives outside of the classroom. However, having students transfer skills and reasoning to new problems is one of the most challenging goals of education and the learning sciences. This chapter explores the literature on examples, problem solving, and interest to offer a simple but effective strategy for improving problem solving.

The Myths

1. Using an example helps students generalize.
2. Examples make the topic interesting.
3. Making the material relatable or interesting automatically leads to learning.

The Research

The entirety of this chapter can be summed up in a very simple rule: two examples are better than one. This may seem obvious at first. Of course multiple examples should be better than one example. However, without understanding the why and how, it can be easy to slip up and make the instructional blunder of only using one example and falling prey to some of the associated myths.

Before directly addressing the myths surrounding examples, it seems appropriate to start off by using an example. Take a break from reading through research and worrying about instructional practice and enjoy a short fairy tale.

Once upon a time there was a small country ruled by a dictator in a strong fortress. There were many roads leading to the fortress at the center of the country. The roads went through the sprawling farms and villages in the countryside. Fed up with the dictator's rule, a general gathered his army. Ready to make a full-scale attack, he amassed his troops at the head of one of the roads. However, just before he ordered his troops to attack, he received word that the dictator had placed bombs on the roads. The bombs were rigged so that very small groups of men could pass over them, thus villagers and farmers were able to use the roads to travel and transport goods, but if a larger group, like an army, passed over them then they would explode, destroying not only the army but the farms and villages as well. The general was a clever man and immediately devised a plan. He ordered his army to split into small groups—small enough so that the bombs would not go off. He then placed these small groups along the many roads and coordinated their arrival at the fortress so that the full army arrived at the same time. The general was able to overtake the fortress and get rid of the dictator.

(adapted from Gick & Holyoak, 1980 (1))

Now that you've had a break, try to solve the following problem:

Pretend you are a doctor with a patient who has a malignant tumor in their stomach. You cannot operate on the patient and remove the tumor, but the tumor is going to kill the patient unless it is destroyed. You know that a high intensity ray will destroy the tumor, but at that intensity it will also kill healthy tissue, which will kill the patient. At a lower intensity that is safe for the healthy tissue, it won't destroy the tumor, which will kill the patient. How can you use the rays to destroy the tumor without destroying the healthy tissue?

(adapted from Duncker, 1945 (2))

On the surface, these two stories may not seem to have much in common. One is about a general and a fortress, the other about a doctor and a tumor. Upon closer inspection, however, there are some significant similarities. Both cannot achieve their objective by attacking directly. In order to solve the doctor's problem with the tumor, you can use the general's solution with the fortress as an example. These are examples from an important paper on analogical problem solving by Gick and Holyoak in the journal *Cognitive Psychology* (1). Across several experiments they found that unless they prompted students to use the fortress story, students ignored the example and tried to come up with a new solution. Only 20 percent of students gave the correct answer—use multiple low intensity rays from different angles. There is good news however; once Gick and Holyoak prompted students to think back to the story then 70 percent of the students were able to solve the problem. This demonstrated two important things. First, the analogy was not difficult to make. Students were able to solve the problem with no directions other than to think back to the story. They didn't need any other detailed analysis or explanation; the example was enough to demonstrate the concept. Second, making the analogy to the example was not automatic. Students needed prompting to make the analogy. The second conclusion is somewhat upsetting for teachers who try to liven up their classrooms with cool and relevant examples. You can't be there to prompt a student to use a relevant example every time they need it.

This creates an interesting problem for teachers. Clearly, examples can be useful. The usefulness, however, is limited by whether or not students remember to use them. Why don't students use relevant examples to help them? Let's examine the process a little bit more closely in our example.

Analogical problem solving refers to the process by which people solve problems that are similar, or analogous, to each other. While there are a number of things that can affect students' problem solving—background knowledge, fluid intelligence, and familiarity with the problem—analogical problem solving focuses specifically on what happens when students are faced with two similar problems: when an example problem can help them solve a new, unfamiliar problem. These problems can be broken down into their **surface details** and their **structural details**. The surface details are often irrelevant for solving the problem, while the structural details are typically about the important processes and properties that are relevant for solving the problem. Often what confuses students about examples is the focus on surface, rather than structural, details (3–5). In other words, when students see the tumor problem, they don't remember the general and the fortress story because it seems so different on the surface. Instead, they think about medical procedures and try to rely on their knowledge of lasers and rays.

Now that we have explained a little bit about how examples and problem solving work, let's revisit some myths about examples.

1. Myth: Using an example helps students generalize

RESEARCH: Students will often focus on, and remember, irrelevant details.

Using examples can help students generalize, but only giving one example can often confuse and distract students. Recall our example above. We first gave you a story about a fortress in the middle of a country and then asked you to solve a medical problem about a patient with a tumor. Rather than generalizing the solution from one to another, most people focus on the new problem and immediately forget about the story they just heard. In the article "Schema induction and analogical transfer," researchers gave students multiple stories before testing them on that tumor problem. Recall that when they gave them one source problem, only 20 percent of students were able to give the correct answer without a hint to think back to that original problem. When they were given two example problems, however, 40–50 percent of students gave the correct answer. Gick and Holyoak theorized that the students' mental model of the problem, their **schema**, was better after reading two similar stories because they were able to see past the surface detail and notice the structural similarities between the two stories. Even better, they found that performance continued to improve—around 60 percent gave the correct answer—when students were provided with a principle or a diagram that helped explain the process at work (3).

Connections

One way to help students form appropriate schemas is to provide visual examples along with text or verbal examples. Diagrams, charts, and pictures can all help students build a better mental representation of a process or concept. These examples are even more effective when they are combined with verbal information explaining and reinforcing what is presented in the picture. Giving both visual and verbal information helps students use **dual coding**. Chapter 5: Learning Styles discusses how dual coding can benefit all learners and explains the concept in more depth.

Part of the key to understanding how students build schemas, how they pick and choose which details to include in their schema and which ones to leave out, is understanding the differences between how novices and experts view problems. Even though it may not always feel like it, as teachers we are the experts in the topics we are teaching. Many key details and relationships that seem obvious to us are simply not obvious to students. As novices they do not know which details are important and which ones are just surface details. The ability to focus on the structural details rather than the surface details comes with practice and experience. For example, when encountering new physics problems the novice student will most likely think about the problems in terms of their surface details—was there a spring, or an inclined plane? The experts, however, will see the problems differently. Experts will categorize problems based on the laws of physics at work, structural details like whether it involves the Conservation of Energy or Newton's Second Law (F = MA) (6). While an example may seem obviously related to what you are discussing in class, a cool example of an underlying principle or process, keep in mind that most novices will focus on the surface details and may miss the structural details you are trying to highlight.

2. Myth: Examples make the topic interesting

RESEARCH: Examples don't always lead to meaningful interest.

A big part of why we include examples is to make learning more fun and interesting, to punch up the lesson a bit with something relatable. When done the right way, these examples liven up a dull lesson and give students the motivation to focus and pay attention. When done the wrong way, however, these examples can distract from the lesson and confuse students.

Using examples to make a topic interesting has the potential to backfire. Instead of fostering an appreciation or deeper understanding of the material, the example may serve to distract from the topic at hand. Students can be drawn in by the seductive details of the example and remember little else. Research on interest and learning distinguishes between two types of interest: **situational interest** and **individual interest** (7). Situational interest is a temporary interest generated by the situation. Waiting at a doctor's office and picking up a magazine that you would not typically read is an example of situational interest. Listening to a funny story about the misapplication of a chemical process, like accidentally making a baking soda volcano in your kitchen while baking, is another example of situational interest. Individual interest, on the other hand, comes from within the individual and not the situation. Individual interest is an enduring characteristic of a person that causes them to respond positively towards a topic and actively seek it out (8–10). Individual interest is the type of interest associated with life-long learners and high-achieving students. Two students listening to the story about baking soda may have different levels of individual interest in chemistry but can both find the situation interesting. While situational interest can lead to individual interest (7), one cool story or example is not enough to inspire an individual interest in a topic. The baking soda story may have inspired interest in that lesson, but it did not necessarily inspire interest in chemistry.

Researchers explain how situational interest can lead to individual interest in the journal *Educational Psychologist* (7). In their "Four-Phase Model of Interest Development" Hidi and Renninger propose that there are four phases of interest:

1. Triggered situational interest
2. Maintained situational interest
3. Emerging individual interest
4. Well-developed individual interest

As we discussed above, interesting examples can lead to situational interest. Situational interest can also be triggered by certain learning environments like group work, puzzles, and computers (7, 11, 12). What distinguishes triggered situational interest from maintained situational interest is persistence and focus. If the situational interest is held during meaningful tasks and in instructional conditions that allow for personal involvement, like project-based learning, cooperative group work, and one-on-one tutoring, then it becomes a maintained situational interest (7, 12). Providing students with an interesting example may trigger their situational interest, but giving them an opportunity to interact with the material in some meaningful way is what leads to maintained situational interest. By maintaining their situational interest through engaging activities and projects, it builds a bridge toward individual interest. Emerging individual interest and well-developed individual interest are distinguished by how long and how enduring the interest in a topic is. Emerging individual interest tends to be self-generated, whereas situational interest is externally supported. In addition, emerging individual interest is associated with knowledge and value about a topic (7, 13, 14). Learning environments can enable the development of individual interest by allowing the student to interact with the knowledge building process (7, 15). The final phase of interest development, well-developed interest, leads to the student being more resourceful, anticipating the next steps, having a feeling of effortlessness when engaging with the material, sustaining long-term constructive and creative endeavors, and developing deeper levels of strategies for work with tasks (7, 16–18). You can deepen a student's well-developed interest by providing them with opportunities to engage with and challenge the material (17).

Often when we talk about student interest in a topic we are really referring to emerging or well-developed individual interest. While examples can trigger situational interest, they are only the first step in developing the more meaningful individual interest. If handled correctly, by creating conditions for maintained situational interest and then emerging individual interest, examples can be an important and memorable first step towards a life-long well-developed interest.

3. Myth: Making the material relatable or interesting automatically leads to learning

> **RESEARCH: If handled inappropriately, interest may confuse and distract from important information.**

It's difficult to separate this myth from the previous myth. Taken together, the myth goes something like "Using examples makes the material more interesting so that students will remember it better." As we discussed above, using an example does not always make the topic more interesting. Using an interesting example may have inspired situational interest, but not individual interest. Furthermore, the interest in the example may actually confuse and distract students from the important material.

Interesting examples often come with a type of surface detail: **seductive details**. Seductive details are details that are both interesting and irrelevant, but nonetheless are remembered more often than other parts of the text or lecture (19, 20). For example, a text explaining how lightning forms might use some details about how lightning is studied to make the passage more interesting: "scientists sometimes create lightning by launching tiny rockets into overhead clouds" (21, 22). This sentence adds some rich description and context to the explanation of how lightning forms. However, when sentences like this are used in texts or lectures, students recall the seductive details at higher rates than the main ideas (21). While adding some interesting facts or details to an example may make it more interesting, that does not guarantee that students will remember it better.

Connections

A common complaint from educators is that students fail to understand a lesson after the teacher has gone out of their way to find an example. This is particularly frustrating when it comes out later in a test or an essay. The student gives an answer that shows the exact wrong interpretation of the right example. *So close, but so far!* One way to avoid this misunderstanding is to provide opportunities for feedback from students early on in the learning process. Don't wait until the test to find out that the perfect, funny, interesting, or relevant example you used was grossly misused and underappreciated by your students. Chapter 4: Testing reviews ways to use retrieval to get feedback from lessons so that misunderstandings can be corrected early.

Interest does not automatically lead to learning because there are different types of interest. As we discussed in the previous myth, there are several steps between interest triggered by a situation and a well-developed interest that drives a student to engage with and challenge material (7). The different types of situational interest are generated by the situation and are not necessarily associated with higher levels of background knowledge and intrinsic motivation from the student. However, activities that encourage students to interact with the material in meaningful ways help students to build an individual interest that is associated with more knowledge and motivation to seek out and re-engage with the topic. Interest can stimulate learning, but it is an ongoing process that instructors can encourage by creating multiple opportunities to engage with the material in meaningful ways.

Connections

When students generate their own examples they are engaging in a form of *retrieval practice* (see Chapter 4: Testing). So not only does this help them learn by providing multiple, different examples of a concept, it helps them remember the concept in the future. Crucially, it helps them remember the concept in similar contexts in the future. One of the biggest challenges in learning and memory is transferring learning from one context to another. Students may be skilled at recognizing main ideas in texts that they read, but may fail to remember the importance of them when they write. By practicing retrieval in this context they increase the chances that they will remember the concept in the future.

Summary

- Multiple examples help students generalize and understand important structural details, instead of irrelevant surface or seductive details.
- Examples can generate interest—but only situational interest, not the more meaningful individual interest.
- Situational interest can be cultivated into individual interest with the appropriate instructional guidance.
- Interest from examples does not automatically lead to learning. Getting students interested is only the first step.

● ● ● ● ●

The Tools

So how can you use interesting examples to improve learning? One easy way is to return to our simple rule: two examples are better than one. Giving just one example makes it difficult for students to figure out what's important. Multiple examples make it easier for students to see the structural similarity between the examples so they can remember and use the concept in the future (3, 4). Another way to improve learning from examples is to provide clear explanations of the structural details. It's not enough to just provide the interesting or relevant example and move on. Students will more than likely only remember those seductive details of the example and in a worst-case scenario they may not even be aware that the example was related to the course material at all. Furthermore, students have different strategies for dealing with examples. Some students tend to try to memorize examples instead of trying to think about the principles or underlying lesson of the example (23). In other words, not all students will try to think deeply about an example. Some students will simply try to memorize the example without connecting it to the material, no matter how interesting or relevant the example is. By clearly and directly explaining why an example is a good demonstration of some concept or process, you can help all students. Ideally, educators would use multiple examples of a concept and explain each example.

Taken as a whole, the research on examples, problem solving, and interest suggests that using examples in lessons can be a powerful tool to motivate students and help them understand deeper concepts. However, simply peppering a lesson with random examples is not enough to inspire interest, learning, or generalization from those examples. By using multiple examples and explaining their connection to the material you can help students learn more while still keeping it interesting.

Early Elementary

- **Use Multiple Examples:** This basic rule can be applied even at the earliest stages of schooling. When explaining or describing a new concept use multiple examples. For example, if students are learning about fractions it is important to give examples of fractions in a variety of different contexts. Sharing a candy bar, pieces of a pie, proportion of marbles, making change from a dollar, etc.
- **Use Different Examples:** In the example above the multiple examples demonstrate slightly different aspects of fractions. Pies and candy bars are whole objects that can be broken into smaller pieces. Marbles are individual units that can be counted out as a portion over the whole set. Finally, money represents something in-between that has to be exchanged to divide up a larger unit into smaller units (i.e. a dollar can be divided into four by exchanging it for four quarters). By exposing students to variations of examples it helps them better understand the underlying concepts.
- **Explain Examples:** Of course, it's not enough to simply explain an example. By clearly explaining *why* an example is a good example of a process you can take away some of the mystery for students who may not pick up on it right away. Remember that as the expert

it may seem obvious to you why one quarter is 1/4th of a dollar, but to a novice, a student, it may not be clear at all.
- **Discuss Student-Generated Examples:** Engage students by asking them to come up with examples of what they are learning in class. Not only does this engage the student coming up with an example, but it provides an additional example for other students. Students can often come up with surprising intuitions and connections that you may not have thought of. This can be incredibly informative for you as the instructor. Students may be simply repeating examples you gave them, or they might come up with great new examples or weird wrong examples. Either way, you learn a bit more about what they have taken away from your lesson. When asking students to generate examples it is important to discuss why their examples are good or bad examples, otherwise they may end up being more confused by seemingly contradictory examples.

Late Elementary

- **Use Multiple Examples:** This basic rule can be applied at all stages of schooling and learning. For example, in late elementary if students are learning about main ideas and supporting ideas in texts it is important to give them a variety of texts to summarize. Students should see examples of main ideas and supporting ideas in texts about science (animals, weather, atoms, etc.), social studies and history (ancient Greece, economics, the Phoenicians, political science, etc.), short stories, and novels.
- **Use Different Examples:** Just as with early elementary, it is important that the multiple examples come from different areas or applications of the concepts. In our example above, this helps students recognize that all expository writing, and most narrative writing, will be structured around main ideas and supporting ideas.
- **Explain Examples:** Similar to early elementary, it is always good practice to explain how a certain example is a good example of the idea you are illustrating.
- **Discuss Student-Generated Examples:** As students learn about more complex topics, their generated examples can become more complex. In the example we are using in this section, main ideas and supporting ideas, students can not only identify how these are used in other texts but they can generate their own writing. By generating their own example of how to use main ideas and supporting ideas students are learning not only to recognize main ideas and supporting ideas, but also how to use them. As with early elementary students, it is important to discuss with students why their example is good or ways in which it can be improved.

Middle School

- **Use Multiple Examples:** While it is still important to include multiple examples in the classroom and the lesson itself, by middle school students are better able to follow directions independently and can be exposed to more examples as they complete worksheets and homework. In algebra, for example, students can work through sets of equations on their own, or in groups.
- **Use Different Examples:** Again, exposing students to a variety of examples helps them better understand the underlying concept. Working through various equations, word problems, and scenarios helps students learn how to apply algebra concepts in multiple contexts, for example. If students only work through equations they may not recognize when or how to use algebra to help them figure out real-world problems. Understanding how to solve $35/2.5 = x$ is one thing; recognizing that if you have $35 dollars to spend on cupcakes for a party and they cost $2.50 and you therefore need to divide 35 by 2.5 to figure out how many you can get is another.
- **Explain Examples:** It is especially important to explain examples as concepts become more abstract and increasingly complicated. There are more ways in which students can misapply a principle or even unknowingly apply a wrong principle. By clearly explaining how and why an example works you help avoid confusion.
- **Discuss Student-Generated Examples:** As with late elementary, students can benefit not only from recognizing and identifying an example but from creating their own. As always it is important to discuss these examples with other students to expose them to more examples, and to also discuss what was good and bad about an example.
- **Corners:** Instructors will place content topics in the corners of the classroom. Students will move to the corner of greatest personal interest. Within the corner, students will form in small groups of two or three. While in the groups students will discuss the topic and why they chose the specific topic. Students will then move to another corner and will have a similar conversation. While in the corner, students will discuss how this new topic relates or differs from the previous topic that they had chosen. This activity will allow students to utilize different content topic examples and determine similarities and differences between each example.

High School and College

- **Use Multiple Examples:** See above.
- **Use Different Examples:** See above.
- **Explain Examples:** See above.

- **Corners:** See above.
- **Discuss Student-Generated Examples:** As discussed above, students can benefit not only from recognizing and identifying an example but from creating their own. It is important both to discuss these examples with other students to expose them to more examples, and also to discuss what was good and bad about an example.

    - *"... in the news":* As students get older and become more media and news savvy, this opens up a new avenue for student-generated examples. An activity to help students learn about a topic in the real world is to ask them to pay attention to news stories about the topic. You might set aside the first five minutes of a world history class for students to report on current events in a country in the region of the world you are studying.
    - *Give 1 to Get 1:* This activity can be used with varied grade levels and in multiple subject areas. The instructor will provide the students with varied reading from a specific topic of focus. Based on the reading, students will complete a provided worksheet that consists of 9 to 12 boxes. The instructor will explain to the students that they will record three of their own ideas about the topic. The students will then move around the classroom to peers who read an alternative reading, the students will discuss their individual readings with peers and will exchange the ideas that they have found. The students must receive one idea from each peer so that each idea is different. The students will complete this process until all of the boxes are filled. This activity provides students with multiple opportunities to compare different texts related to a similar topic, allows students to learn from one another, and allows students to be active listeners.

● ● ● ● ●

References

1. Gick M & Holyoak KJ (1980) Analogical problem solving. *Cognitive Psychology* 12:306–355.
2. Duncker K (1945) On problem solving. *Psychological Monographs* 58(Whole No. 270).
3. Gick M & Holyoak KJ (1983) Schema induction and analogical transfer. *Cognitive Psychology* 15:1–38.
4. Holyoak KJ (2012) Analogy and relational reasoning. *Oxford handbook of thinking and reasoning*, ed. Morrison KJHRG (Oxford University Press, New York), pp 234–259.
5. Kubricht JR, Lu H, & Holyoak KJ (2017) Individual differences in spontaneous analogical transfer. *Memory & Cognition* 45:576–588.
6. Chi MTH, Feltovich PJ, & Glaser R (1981) Categorization and representation of physics problems by experts and novices. *Cognitive Science* 5(2):121–152.

7. Hidi S & Renninger KA (2006) The four-phase model of interest development. *Educational Psychologist* 41(2):111–127.
8. Durik AM & Harackiewicz JM (2007) Different strokes for different folks: How personal interest moderates the effects of situational factors on task interest. *Journal of Educational Psychology* 99:597–610.
9. Hidi S & Harackiewicz JM (2000) Motivating the academically unmotivated: A critical issue for the 21st century. *Review of Educational Research* 70(2):151–179.
10. Schiefele U (1991) Interest, learning, and motivation. *Educational Psychologist* 26(2 & 3):299–323.
11. Cordova DI & Lepper MR (1996) Intrinsic motivation and the process of learning: Beneficial effects of contextualization, personalization, and choice. *Journal of Educational Psychology* 88:715–730.
12. Hidi S, Weiss J, Berndorff D, & Nolan J (1998) The role of gender, instruction and a cooperative learning technique in science education across formal and informal settings. *Interest and learning: Proceedings of the Seeon conference on interest and gender*, ed. L. Hoffman AK, KA Renninger & J Baumert (IPN, Kiel, Germany), pp 215–227.
13. Bloom B (1985) The nature of the study and why it was done. *Developing talent in young people*, ed. Bloom B (Ballantine, New York), pp 3–18.
14. Renninger KA (2000) Individual interest and its implications for understanding motivation. *Intrinsic and extrinsic motivation: The search for optimal motivation and performance*, ed. Harackiewicz CSJM (Academic, New York), pp 375–407.
15. Hoffmann L (2002) Promoting girls' learning and achievement in physics classes for beginners. *Learning and Instruction* 12:447–465.
16. Izard CE & Acherman BP (2000) Organizational, and regulatory functions of discrete emotions. *Handbook of emotions*, ed. Haviland-Jone MLJM (Guildford, New York), 2 Ed, pp 253–264.
17. Renninger KA & Shumar W (2002) Community building with and for teachers: The Math Forum as a resource for teacher professional development. *Building virtual communities: Learning and change in cyberspace*, ed. Shumar KARW (Cambridge University Press, New York), pp 60–95.
18. Alexander PA & Murphy PK (1998) Profiling the differences in students' knowledge, interest, and strategic processing. *Journal of Educational Psychology* 90:435–447.
19. Garner R, Gillingham MG, & White CS (1989) Effects of "seductive details" on macroprocessing and microprocessing in adults and children. *Cognition and Instruction* 6:41–57.
20. Harp SF & Maslich AA (2005) The consequences of including seductive details during lecture. *Teaching of Psychology* 32:100–103.
21. Lehman S, Schraw G, McCrudden MT, & Hartley K (2007) Processing and recall of seductive details in scientific text. *Contemporary Educational Psychology* 32(4):569–587.
22. Harp SF & Mayer RE (1998) How seductive details do their damage: A theory of cognitive interest in science learning. *Journal of Educational Psychology* 90(3):414–434.
23. Little JL & McDaniel MA (2015) Individual differences in category learning: Memorization versus rule abstraction. *Memory & Cognition* 43(2):283–297.

3

Focus

Focus is often referred to as **selective attention** by researchers. Selective attention is the skill of ignoring distracting stimuli. While research shows that we have some individual innate differences in our ability to control our attention the research also reveals that we can improve this control of attention with practice. Mirroring the chapter on multitasking, we outline why practicing selective attention to ignore distractions is essential to maintaining concentration and attention to the task at hand. The scientific literature speaks to two important facts. First, a general lack of control over limited attentional resources is one of the biggest problems for deep thinking. Second, several factors contribute to our ability/skill to focus. Exercising focus over time helps us stay on task. In other words, selective attention, or focus, is the instrument used to avoid the distractions we talked about in Chapter 1: Multitasking.

The Myths

1. The ability to focus is inborn: some people have it, some people don't.
2. The best way to improve focus on real-world tasks is to avoid distractions by finding a quiet area with nothing to distract you.
3. I can still focus, even with my cell phone.
4. Getting distracted and letting your mind wander isn't a big deal.

The Research

Attention is a crucial first step in the learning process. The ability to focus, to orient our attention, determines what gets targeted for learning and memory (1). Once our attention has been oriented to information, selective attention (focus) directly affects how well the information is learned or remembered (2). It does this by reducing irrelevant information and attempts to maximize your attentional resources for processing. Research has found that focusing attention to avoid distractions has strong associations with academic success (3). Selective attention is critical for academic success because it determines how well a student can ignore distractions and pay attention to important information.

1. Myth: The ability to focus is inborn: some people have it, some people don't

RESEARCH: Being able to focus (selectively attend) is a skill that can be improved over time.

In Chapter 1: Multitasking we talked about how performance increases when people stick to one task versus multitasking. We reviewed an article from *Frontiers in Human Neuroscience* that showed that people scored best in the single-tasking condition, followed closely by the selective attention condition (4). In the selective attention condition there were both visual and auditory distractors, but the participant was told to ignore the distracting stimuli. If we look again, this time focusing on the selective attention group we see that when people are motivated and instructed to ignore distractors, they can. While performance was not as good as the single-tasking group, willfully ignoring distractors made performance better than the multitasking group.

Further evidence that selective attention can be improved is revealed by research on training of attentional control. Specifically, we see very effective results from process-based training (5). Of crucial importance is that this type of training shows reliable transfer of these newly gained skills to novel tasks. Selective attention has been shown to improve substantially with motivational factors including performance rewards. With this preliminary evidence we can be reassured that the ability to ignore distractions can be helped considerably. Cognitive training to control attentional focus works for children, adolescents, young adults, and older adults (5, 6).

Connections

One of the prevailing theories in attention describes how subjects only encode what is task-relevant and filter out other details that are irrelevant. For example, in one experiment, even though subjects selectively attended to a ball for 30 seconds, they were not able to report the color of the ball because they were not expecting to report the color (7). In expectancy-based binding "we propose that information that is expected to be useful later is more likely to be bound to the object representation in working memory" (7, p. 147). Here, the ball was attended to so the information gets stored, however, non-relevant information about the task seems to be thrown to the wayside, and only what they feel is important remains in working memory. Chapter 2: Examples explains that more examples are better because students are more likely to understand the concept. However, in many cases it may be best for teachers to explicitly tell the students what to selectively attend to.

Development

Preschool children have difficulties both with selective attention and with task switching. However, as children develop and start to enter kindergarten they become better at both selectively attending to, or switching attention to different components of an item, like color or shape. Researchers suggests that the two developmental processes may have a common underlying cause (8).

Research has demonstrated in adolescents that focus can be greatly improved with motivation (9, 10). Not only does cognitive training in childhood and adolescence improve selective attention, but the benefits from the training are, most importantly, transferable to separate tasks (11). This research is important because it shows that children can improve their focus through training.

2. Myth: The best way to improve focus on real-world tasks is to avoid distractions by finding a quiet area with nothing to distract you

> ***RESEARCH: Practicing focus of attention with distractions around you improves focus over time.***

Perhaps you know people who cannot think clearly when craziness is happening all around them. Perhaps you are one of those people. Realize that this is not necessarily "the type of person you are," but rather that people need practice focusing their attention in those situations. If you want to be able to think clearly and focus in your hectic and distracting everyday life it helps to practice this skill in the same environment.

One reason to practice improving selective attention is that improved focus helps us to avoid multitasking. The lack of focus helps explain why students are so prone to distraction. Students who have not developed the skill to ignore distractions are, in essence, unable to stop themselves from multitasking. People tend to multitask because they are unable to filter out and/or cognitively avoid distraction (12).

When we cannot ignore distractions, it hurts our productivity. Wendt et al. (13) asked people to complete tasks in the presence of distractions. Unsurprisingly, they found that distractions harm the productivity of completing the tasks. But when are distractions most harmful? As reported in the *Journal of Experimental Psychology* (14) "high load on processes of cognitive control such as working memory and task coordination leads to increased distractor interference" (p. 351). This tells us that thinking processes with many steps are more susceptible to distraction. One of the most important things to be aware of in your classroom are those times when students are learning a complex set of steps or stages. At those times it helps students to have as few distractions as possible or to be able to ignore those distractions.

The good news is that we can train our attention and improve our focus. Current research is very clear on the point and it is well documented that attentional focus can be improved at any age through training and practice (15). Additionally, concerning attentional focus, researchers note that "[p]eople improve on the skills they practice and that transfers to other contexts where those same skills are needed, but people *only* improve on what they practice; improvement does not seem to transfer to other skills" (p. 57). This last point, that training generalizes to other contexts, is crucial. This means that training on selective attention in one context, like a classroom activity, has the ability to improve selective attention in general. Using activities that improve students' focus and selective attention are worthwhile because they will actually get better at that skill, not just better at the activity.

3. Myth: I can still focus, even with my cell phone

RESEARCH: Cell phones are designed to attract your attention, and research demonstrates that attention and learning are systematically harmed in several ways by mobile devices.

Whether in the classroom, driving down the highway, or studying at home, cell phones may be the biggest single factor in loss of attention, memory and learning. While smartphones are wonderful devices, giving us access to limitless information, mountains of social media, games, videos, texts, tweets, instagrams and much, much more, they also are a major factor in distracting children, adolescents, and adults from some extremely important activities like driving, studying, and paying attention in class (for a review see Chen & Yan, 2016 (16)).

Studies have shown that both your cell phone notifications, and others' cell phone notifications have drastic effects on memory. When a cell phone noise goes off, everyone in the room will be distracted and attempt to figure out where the noise came from (17). More mistakes are made in the presence of cell phones. Cell phone notifications (text or call) greatly decrease the ability to perform well on attention-based tasks. This is due to the notification forcing attention to task-irrelevant thoughts, which continue after the notification. What is more startling is that this happens whether or not the person picks up the phone or reads the message (18).

In an article titled "The impact of mobile phone usage on student learning," researchers reveal several very interesting conclusions about the relationship between cell phones and classrooms. They found that there was a negative relationship between texting/posting and test scores, as texting/posting increased, test scores dropped. Results also indicate that texting/posting decreases the total amount of note taking. Compared to students who did not use a cell phone in class, students who had a high level of cell phone use in class recalled 51 percent less of the material (19).

Bottom line: *cell phone use distracts us, and those around us.* Keep this in mind for all of your activities, when deciding whether or not to allow cell phones in your classroom, and when you are studying, or your child is studying. Because cell phones are designed to attract your attentional focus, distracting you from other activities, they force task switching (multitasking). By forcing task switching they lead to all of the bad outcomes for attention, memory and learning described in Chapter 1: Multitasking. When it is time to learn, power off your cell phone, and leave it in another room. When you are done studying your connection to the outside world can be powered back up and you can reward yourself for a job well done. The job: Focusing.

4. Myth: Getting distracted and letting your mind wander isn't a big deal

> **RESEARCH: *Distractions and mind wandering hurt your attention, learning, and memory more than you think.***

It's no surprise that despite our best efforts, our minds wander from time to time. While the occasional daydream or planning out your day is inevitable, you may not be aware of the negative impact it has on your attention and learning. In a 2016 study published in the journal *Memory & Cognition*, participants reported that they were on task 54 percent of the time and off task/mind-wandering 27 percent of the time (20). Researchers found that accuracy on the task was lower if the participant(s) had noted that they were mind-wandering. For the participants who said that they were mind-wandering during the tasks, their overall performance on those tasks was lower compared to the participants who did not mind-wander (20). Furthermore, when people are distracted they remember less and feel less confident in their responses to questions compared to people who are not distracted (21). This research tells us that people tend to know when they are distracted, perform worse when they are distracted, and feel less confident when completing tasks while distracted. Furthermore, distractions hurt us more if they happen during a difficult task (22). Getting distracted while completing a relatively simple task like folding laundry isn't as big a deal as getting distracted while performing more complicated tasks, like studying for a tough exam or driving a car.

Part of what makes something distracting is how similar or different it is to the task we are focusing on. In an interesting article from the *Journal of Experimental Psychology: Human Perception and Performance*, researchers found that when we focus, or selectively attend to something, and the distractor is related in some way to that thing, we are more easily distracted. Alternatively, if the distractor is very different from what we are trying to focus on, we will be less easily distracted (23).

Connections

This research on distraction and selective attention highlights the bottleneck in learning: attentional resources. In order to learn new information we must pay attention to it in order to move it to long-term memory. The more **cues** that are attached to the piece of information, the more likely it is to be remembered later (see Chapter 4: Testing). Your ability to focus and ignore distracting information either helps to maximize the number of items you can hold in attention or hurts it by reducing the number of task-relevant items held in attention. People who can focus and have more attentional resources can associate more cues with the new information, helping them to remember it later. People who get distracted and have fewer attentional resources have fewer cues with new information, hurting their memory.

Summary

- Selective attention directly affects how well information is learned.
- Focusing is a skill that can be improved with practice.

- Focusing often increases academic success.
- In some cases, especially with young children, it may be best to tell the students what to focus on.
- For better focus in distracting environments, practice in distracting environments.
- Cell phones distract us and those around us and are associated with poor academic performance.
- Distractions harm learning.

The Tools

Selective attention refers to the skill of focusing on a task, activity, or information while blocking out distracting stimuli. Activities that encourage selective attention and single tasking are anything that has only one activity going on at a time. Encourage students to improve their selective attention by structuring activities that encourage them to stay on task.

Early Elementary

- **Check-Ins:** Throughout a lesson, continuing to "check in" with students. Ask important and relevant questions about the material. These should not be trick questions. These are simply an attention check. If the student is paying attention to the lesson and relevant material these should not come as surprises or difficult to answer questions.
- **In Your Own Words:** During periods of individual or group work sessions, ask the student to explain why they are doing what they are doing. Ask them to explain in their own words why they have decided to approach the problem the way they have.
- **Brain Break:** During the instruction period, allow for structured pauses in the presentation of material. This provides the students with an opportunity to get up, stretch out, or simply break from constantly focusing on material. This technique has been shown to prolong students' ability to focus over longer periods of time.

Late Elementary

- **Teacher-Centered Direct Instruction:** This method of instruction requires that students focus their attention on the presenter and the material that is relevant to the topic. If students do not focus their attention they will misunderstand material. This is a more straightforward approach to commanding focus and attention.

Middle School

- **Done/Yet To Do Questions:** While working in small groups, the instructor will ask students to determine what assignments the group has completed, tasks that have not been completed yet, and to determine what else needs to be completed. While in the groups, the students will determine what tasks still need to be completed, how those tasks will get completed and what methods will be used to complete these tasks.
- **Finger Minute:** While working on an activity, the instructor will instruct the students to pause and evaluate how much progress they have made on the assignment. The instructor will then advise the groups to discuss with the group members how many minutes they require to complete the task and designate one person to raise his or her hand to indicate how many minutes the group needs to finish. Based on the student responses, the instructor will determine an average time to provide the students. This method will allow the instructor to determine how the students are doing on the task and provides the students with reinforcement to stay on task and an amount of time.
- **Modeling:** This technique works by providing students with a visual of what it is that they are to do. Having a visual representation of the steps involved in completing a task allows for students to focus on the relevant tools and information for effectively completing a task.

High School and College

- **Done/Yet To Do Questions:** See above.
- **Modeling:** See above.
- **5–3–1:** This activity should be conducted repeatedly after lessons and instruction. The students will be separated into small groups of four to five students. The instructor will instruct members to identify five words that represent topics or content gained from the lesson. The group members will share their ideas in a round-robin fashion. While in the group, members will discuss the ideas that peers present. The groups will then determine three central ideas that they have gained from the lesson. The students will then determine what the label for these three ideas would be. This activity will allow students to remember concepts and topics that were gained from the lesson as well as allowing the students to acknowledge specific parts of the content.

● ● ● ● ●

References

1. Ross-Sheehy S, Oaks LM, & Luck SJ (2011) Exogenous attention influences visual short-term memory in infants. *Developmental Science* 14:490–501.
2. Markant J & Amso D (2014) Leveling the playing field: Attention mitigates the effects of intelligence on memory. *Cognition* 131:195–204.
3. Howard S, Johnson JL, & Pascual-Leone J (2014) Clarifying inhibitory control: Diversity and development of attentional inhibition. *Cognitive Development* 31:1–21.
4. Moisala M, Salmela V, Salo E, *et al.* (2015) Brain activity during divided and selective attention to auditory and visual sentence comprehension tasks. *Frontiers in Human Neuroscience* 19:1–15.
5. Karbach J & Verhaeghen P (2014) Making working memory work: A meta-analysis of executive control and working memory training in younger and older adults. *Psychological Science* 24(11):2027–2037.
6. Karbach J & Unger K (2014) Executive control training from middle childhood to adolescence. *Frontiers in Psychology* 5.
7. Chen H, Swan G, & Wyble B (2016) Prolonged focal attention without binding: Tracking a ball for half a minute without remembering its color. *Cognition* 147:144–148.
8. Hanania R & Smith LB (2010) Selective attention and attention switching: Toward a unified developmental approach. *Developmental Science* 13(4):622–635.
9. Kohls G, Peltzer J, Herpetz-Dahlmann B, & Konrad K (2009) Differential effects of social and non-social reward on response inhibition in children and adolescents. *Developmental Science* 12:614–625.
10. Geier CF, Terwilliger R, Teslovich T, Velanova K, & Luna B (2010) Immaturities in reward processing and its influence on inhibitory control in adolescence. *Cerebral Cortex* 20:1613–1629.
11. Miyake A & Friedman NP (2012) The nature and organization of individual differences in executive functions for general conclusions. *Current Directions in Psychological Science* 21:8–14.
12. Ophir E, Nass C, & D. WA (2009) Cognitive control in media multitaskers. *PNAS* 106(37):15583–15587.
13. Wendt M, Kiesel A, Mathew H, Luna-Rodriquez A, & Jacobsen T (2013) Irrelevant stimulus processing when switching between tasks. *Zeitschrift fur Psychologie* 221(1):41–50.
14. Lavie N, Hirst A, Fockert JW, & Viding E (2004) Load theory of selective attention and cognitive control. *Journal of Experimental Psychology: General* 133(3):339–354.
15. Diamond A & Ling D (2016) Conclusions about interventions, programs, and approaches for improving executive functions that appear justified and those that, despite much hype, do not. *Developmental Cognitive Neuroscience* 18:34–48.
16. Chen Q & Yan Z (2016) Does multitasking with mobile phones affect learning? A review. *Computers in Human Behavior* 54:34–42.
17. Roer JP, Bell R, & Buchner A (2014) Please silence your cell phone: Your ringtone captures other people's attention. *Noise & Health* 16(68):34–39.
18. Stothart C, Mitchum A, & Yenhert C (2015) The attentional cost of receiving a cell phone notification. *Journal of Experimental Psychology: Human Perception and Human Performance* 41(4):893–897.

19. Kuznekoff JH & Titsworth S (2013) The impact of mobile phone usage on student learning. *Communication Education* 62(3):233–252.
20. Unsworth N & Robinson MK (2016) The influence of lapses of attention on working memory capacity. *Memory & Cognition* 44:188–196.
21. Sauer J & Hope L (2016) The effects of divided attention at study and reporting procedure on regulation and monitoring for episodic recall. *Acta Psychologica* 169:143–156.
22. Adler RF & Benbunan-Fich R (2014) The effects of task difficulty and multitasking on performance. *Interacting with Computers* 27(4):430–439.
23. Park S, Chun MM, & Kim K (2007) Concurrent working memory load can facilitate selective attention: Evidence for specialized load. *Journal of Experimental Psychology: Human Perception and Human Performance* 33(5):1062–1075.

4

Testing

One of the most powerful and effective ways that we can encourage learning is to give students the opportunity to demonstrate their knowledge and skills, celebrate their successes, and recognize their mistakes. This chapter examines testing and the cognitive mechanism behind it: retrieval practice, how it works, and how it can be used in the classroom.

The Myths

1. Testing only rewards test-taking skills and doesn't actually help students learn.
2. Testing promotes teaching to the test.
3. Testing doesn't actually measure learning.
4. There are two types of students: bad test takers and good test takers.
5. Testing causes undue anxiety and distress that is harmful to students.

The Research

Where did I put my keys? If you're like most people, you have asked yourself this question more recently and more frequently than you would like. In moments of frustration you may have cursed your faulty memory and wished for a better one. We get frustrated with our imperfect memories and our inability to access information that we know we have. Many of us have yelled at our computers for not finding what we want, and our memory seems even worse. We get frustrated that our memories don't return the right search results even when we've entered our best search terms (e.g. "That guy from the one movie with the hair? He's tall."). Why don't our memories work as well as computers? The answer, of course, is that our memory is not like a computer. It's better.

Our memories work by forming complex associations between cues present in our environments and target information stored in our brain (1, 2). **Cues** include anything that triggers a memory, which is the target. A person's face should be a cue to recall their name (the target information). A question on the exam should be a cue to recall the appropriate answer. A song lyric might be the cue to recall an important event (your first date). What makes some cues better at making us remember target information than others? Why is some information easier to access? The more often we have recalled information with a cue in the past helps determine how easy it is for us to recall that information with that cue in the future.

This part of memory makes more sense if you consider what memory is used for. While most people might think that memory is used for remembering the past, learning and memory researchers have actually argued that memory helps us predict the future (3). Our memory system takes into account complex patterns based on the environment, context, and frequency, that help generate the best possible target with the information it has (4). Information that doesn't get used very often is forgotten, unless it was associated with an emotionally-charged, and therefore, a very important event. Information that is used frequently is readily at hand. Consider for a moment what it would be like if your memory system was not selective. If every time you heard the word "mug" you thought of every mug you had ever encountered: coffee mugs, tea mugs, mug shots, ugly mugs, etc. You would then need to consciously consider each option before deciding which mug was most relevant in the current situation. By conveniently forgetting the bulk of the mugs you have ever encountered, your memory system saves you time and energy in everyday conversations. It lets you remember the blue mug that you use for coffee at work instead of the mug shot that went with a news article you read last week.

A simpler way of stating the memory process described above is that memory becomes better the more you use it. Practice makes perfect. Learning and memory researchers study testing as a way to practice memory and examine what factors improve our memory. Learning and memory researchers who study testing mostly focus on the process of **retrieval**. Retrieval is the process of rebuilding a memory in order to call information to mind. Every time something is recalled and students go through the process of retrieval, they get better at rebuilding the memory, making it easier to remember the information in the future (5, 6).

There are a few things to keep in mind when trying to improve memory and learning for a certain set of information. One important aspect of the retrieval process is that it is **cue-dependent** (7). The more times we associate the cue "hola" with the word "hello" the easier and faster it is for us to remember that "hola" means "hello." This cue-dependent nature means that if we learn information in one context, it can be difficult for us to recall it in other contexts. When students study it is most beneficial for them to study in ways that are similar to how they will be tested on the information. If art students are going to be tested on knowledge of color theory and linear perspective by creating a piece of artwork, then simply memorizing the definitions of color theory and linear perspective will be less helpful than practicing drawing or identifying those elements in other pieces of artwork.

Another important aspect of retrieval is that it is a process. For example, take a few seconds to solve the following math problem: 2 x 3 + 4 x 10 = ? If you are a bit rusty on your algebra you may first take a second to remember something about order of operations. Once you have remembered that you need to first multiply 2 x 3 and 4 x 10 to get 6 and 40, then you can add 6 and 40 to come up with an answer of 46. Now that you have brushed up on your algebra skills, attempt a second problem: 2 x 3 + 4 x 10 = ? Was the second problem easier to solve? Did you go through the same process to solve it as you did the first one? Probably not. You didn't have to apply the same steps because it was obviously the same equation as before. Retrieval works a lot like this. Things can be easier to remember if you retrieve them immediately after seeing them or if you retrieve them over and over again, one right after the other. However, you don't get as much benefit from this type of retrieval because you didn't have to go through the same process. This is a roundabout way of explaining what most teachers already know: cramming doesn't work for the long term. Cramming the night before, or minutes before, might give you a short boost, but spacing out your studying and preparing in advance gives you a stronger grasp of the material (8, 9).

Finally, perhaps the most important aspect of retrieval is that it is *not* a neutral learning event. Retrieval is an active process that changes learning. While we use tests, quizzes, practicums, etc. to assess learning, by asking students to retrieve knowledge we are changing their ability to retrieve that knowledge in the future. We are strengthening connections between cues and memories. If you want your students to learn something because it's a useful life skill, then they should practice and be tested in real-world scenarios. If you think basic math is important for balancing a checkbook, for example, then set up a small token economy where they may earn tokens for good behavior and spend them to receive prizes and rewards. Students can keep track of their current supply of tokens in a checkbook. While activities like this make the task more meaningful, they also take away some of the challenges that students have when they need to transfer what they learned in class to actual real-world skills. On the other hand, if you know that certain types of questions are likely to show up on an AP exam, then using those types of questions in study materials and in tests and quizzes in your classroom can increase the chances that students will remember the material in that context on the AP exam.

Now that we have explained a bit about how retrieval works, we can go through some of the research addressing the five teaching and learning myths about testing.

1. Myth: Testing only rewards test-taking skills and doesn't actually help students learn

> **RESEARCH:** *Testing can be one of the most powerful ways to improve learning, if used the right way.*

Testing is one way you can ask students to retrieve knowledge. There are different kinds of tests for different materials and situations—short answer, essay, practicum, research paper, timed drill, laboratory exercise, and, yes, the much-loathed standardized, multiple-choice exam. Most myths and criticisms about tests are referring specifically to multiple-choice exams. Before detailing some of the research that deals specifically with how retrieval improves learning, we should note that there is a wealth of research that says that not all multiple-choice exams are created equal. A multiple-choice exam can be as easy or as challenging, as well-crafted or as poorly-constructed as you would like. Multiple-choice exams can ask simple verbatim questions, asking students to remember a definition straight from the book, or they can ask transfer questions that require students to transfer what they have learned and apply it in a new context (10). Multiple-choice questions can have choices that make the answer obvious, or that have several plausible choices, making the student apply certain criteria to choose the best possible answer (11). The research on multiple-choice tests demonstrates that multiple-choice is not inherently bad or good. There are plenty of very bad multiple-choice tests that do very little to assess learning appropriately. However, there are also plenty of very good multiple-choice tests that are well-crafted to assess learning appropriately.

Retrieval is the single most effective tool for learning that students and teachers have in their arsenal. Retrieval—and therefore testing—as a learning tool is incredibly powerful. While there are undoubtedly issues surrounding standardized tests, high-stakes exams, and rampant misuse of poorly designed tests, the idea that all tests are bad or not relevant to learning is an outright lie. Tests improve later retention of material (12, 13). Tests do not simply assess learning. As of the date of publication of this book there is no way to read another person's mind to assess what they do and do not know. All tests require students to retrieve and produce knowledge in some way because memory is an active process. As an active process, testing can dramatically improve student learning. For example, in an important study in the journal *Psychological Science,* researchers found that students who reread material forgot over half (52 percent) of the material a week later, whereas students who practiced retrieval only forgot 15–30 percent of the material (13).

Retrieval practice is even more effective when it is repeated and spaced out (14, 15). Think of a student being told they need to get a vocabulary word correct at least three times before putting it aside. What should the student do? Should they practice recalling the word three times in a row (massed practice)? Should they space it out, and if so, what spacing is best? Should they space it evenly throughout the study session so that they are recalling it at regular intervals (equal spacing)? Or is it better to recall the word at longer and longer intervals as they get better at recalling it (expanding spacing)? Researchers examined these questions in a study published in the *Journal of Experimental Psychology: Learning, Memory, and Cognition.* They had students study word pairs (similar to using flashcards to learn a set of vocabulary words) in a variety of study conditions. When students' memory was tested a week later researchers found that regardless of the type of spacing—expanding, equal, or contracting—students recalled more (49 percent correct) than if they had not used any spacing—retrieving once or massed practice (26 percent and 25 percent correct). In fact, there was no difference between massed practice and retrieving once! Retrieving a word three times in a row provides no extra benefit over retrieving it once. When students only studied the words once, they performed the worst, on average only recalling 1 percent of the words one week later. However, as soon as spacing was introduced in retrieval practice, students remembered almost twice as much (8).

Not only does spacing improve retrieval practice, the longer retrieval practice is spaced out, the better. In the same study from the *Journal of Experimental Psychology: Learning, Memory, and Cognition,* researchers compared overall length of spacing schedules. They found a substantial benefit of longer spacings. Students recalled 49 percent of the words at shorter spacings, 64 percent of the words at medium spacing, and 75 percent of the words at long spacing (8). As a whole, this research has some practical implications. First, when students are studying they should practice retrieval to improve long-term retention. Second, any spacing between retrieval practice provides a benefit over no spacing and, in fact, the longer the spacing the better. Finally, the pattern of the spacing doesn't seem to matter so the easiest way to use this advice is to make sure that some type of spacing is used to help your memory.

Ultimately retrieval is always more effective when it is done multiple times and when it is spaced out. Retrieving something multiple times in a row without spacing it out is no better than retrieving it only once. Remember the math problem from the beginning of the chapter? The first time you had to go through the steps to solve it, but the second time it was presented you more than likely just repeated the same answer without going through the steps. Spacing out retrieval practice makes you go through the process of retrieval, giving you practice at that process to help you remember things in the future. For example, take a few seconds to solve the following math problem: $2 \times 3 + 4 \times 10 = ?$ You may not have been much faster than the first time you saw this problem, but you also probably found it a bit more difficult than when you were asked to solve it for the second time at the beginning of the chapter.

Another way to get the benefits of spaced retrieval is to use *interleaving* (16). Interleaving is when students switch between ideas during a study session. This can be as simple as shuffling flashcards, working through a worksheet that uses different types of math problems, or studying for a world history exam after reviewing material from a world literature class. Interleaving has been found to be more effective at improving memory than simply spacing out retrieval practice (17, 18). Mixing materials is more effective than just spacing out retrieval because, according to Rohrer (16), "it makes it easier for learners to compare and contrast members of one category with members of a different category. Specifically, members of one category (e.g., finches) might differ from members of another category (e.g., sparrows) in a number of dimensions, and the juxtaposition of two members from different categories helps learners appreciate which dimensions (or features) are most relevant to the task of discrimination" (p. 4). By practicing retrieval with different concepts it makes it easier for students to compare and contrast ideas.

Connections

When using interleaving it is important to be mindful of how long students are on each idea or task. If you are switching between ideas too rapidly then you will experience the drawbacks of task switching described in Chapter 1: Multitasking. To be clear, interleaving requires students to focus on one set of material at a time, only moving on to the next set of material after being given enough time to focus on the material.

Retrieval improves learning directly, as described above, but it also improves learning indirectly. Retrieval helps students identify gaps in knowledge and learn more from their next study session (19–21). Pre-tests and small quizzes leading up to bigger tests can be useful because they can help students identify what they need to study. Not only can retrieval identify gaps, but it can also help students see if they have been overconfident in their abilities and give them a more accurate feel for how much they think they know. In other words, it can improve their metacognition (13). Retrieval can help students organize their knowledge, giving them a structure or system to help with future learning (22, 23). Retrieval improves transfer of knowledge to new contexts by the simple fact that it is easier to transfer something that you can remember and understand than something you can barely even recognize (24–26).

2. Myth: Testing promotes teaching to the test

RESEARCH: *Testing can be a useful tool to help teachers get feedback and adapt materials in real time.*

One of the most overlooked aspects of testing is how it can be used to help the teacher. Not all tests have to be high-stakes, once-a-year tests. In fact, retrieval is most useful when it is spread out in low-stakes games or quizzes (27, 28). Not only do these frequent retrieval attempts help students for all of the reasons listed above, they help with formative assessments, checking each student for mastery toward learning outcomes or objectives, and provide data to guide instruction (13, 29). Quick quizzes or review games can let an instructor see what material students are struggling with, without piling additional grading or prep work on the instructor. This makes retrieval activities—quick quizzes, frequent tests, quiz-games, etc.—ideal for differentiated instruction. At the end of the chapter we will provide a list of suggestions of activities that can be easily integrated into a lesson to check the pulse of the class to see how they're doing. Again, the benefit of these types of activities is at least twofold: the retrieval practice is an active process that improves learning and lets you evaluate the strengths and weaknesses of each student.

3. Myth: Testing doesn't measure learning

RESEARCH: *The ability of a test to measure learning depends on the design of the test and the goals of the learning.*

We have already touched on this myth, but it's such an important point that it's worth addressing this myth specifically. Tests are *not* neutral events and they are *not* inherently bad. The ability of a test to measure learning depends on the design of the test and what the instructor feels the goal of the learning should be. Researchers refer to this as the **validity** of the test. Test validity is the extent to which a test accurately measures what it is supposed to measure. There are many different test formats that can be used to assess even more types of materials and learning situations. Typically when people say that a certain test doesn't measure learning, they actually mean that the test isn't valid. This is an entirely fair criticism to make. There are tests that are appropriate in some situations but not others. For example, a doctor's MCAT score may not be a valid measure of her or his bedside manner, which is an important and relevant aspect of being a doctor. Furthermore, an MCAT score may not be a valid measure of a doctor's ability to make snap judgments in an ER. Both of these are reasons why doctors have to serve as residents after going through their course work. Clearly multiple-choice exams can't measure everything. But at the end of the day, knowing nothing else about them, would you rather have a doctor who scored in the lowest 10 percent of their class on the MCAT or the highest 10 percent? We're willing to bet you'd go with the highest 10 percent. Multiple-choice exams can't measure everything, but they certainly measure something.

Tests are neither all good nor all bad. Instead tests can vary in their validity. Sometimes they can be very good indicators of learning, sometimes they can be very poor indicators of learning. If you have been frustrated with poor tests in the past, don't throw up your hands and throw out tests altogether. Think carefully about what kind of learning you want to reinforce and what tests are appropriate for that learning. For example if you are teaching your students Spanish, then having regular vocabulary quizzes is probably necessary. However, being able to use the vocabulary in a conversation is a little more nuanced than simply recalling that "hola" means "hello." In addition to vocab quizzes you would most likely assign conversation exercises and test students by having them greet you in Spanish every day. By making sure tests align with content, the tests can serve as powerful reinforcers to the content students are learning.

4. Myth: There are two types of students: bad test takers and good test takers

> **RESEARCH: *Test taking is a skill that can be improved in all students.***

This myth is similar to our third myth—testing doesn't measure learning. Instead of focusing on the test, this myth focuses on the student. However, the core of this criticism is the same—some tests are not valid. If you suspect that a large number of students are failing a test despite knowing the material being tested, then it is very possible that the test is not valid.

To be clear, there are other reasons why a student may not do well on a test, aside from simply not knowing the material or the test being poorly designed. Students come into the classroom with a wide range of developmental and learning abilities as well as general test-taking skills. This is different from saying they are bad test takers, however. Blaming poor performance on being a "bad test taker" rather than a diagnosed learning disability, or a lack of experience with taking a certain kind of test, suggests that the student cannot change. It suggests that the world is divided into two types of students: good test takers and bad test takers. It ignores the capability of students to practice and improve at a skill, the fundamental process of retrieval, and encourages bad test takers to feel hopeless when confronted with tests (10, 30–34).

Development

Younger students are not as practiced with tests and may need some extra help with retrieval practice to help them learn. Researchers report in the journal *Frontiers* that children as young as ten years old can benefit from retrieval practice in the classroom (10). However, getting the information right on the first retrieval attempt is important to reinforce learning. Therefore, to help the younger children retrieve information the researchers gave them extra hints and instructed them to think back to what they studied (10). Other research has found that feedback can help improve retrieval in younger students (30, 31). Importantly, in experiments that used vocabulary learning to investigate retrieval practice, the effect of retrieval practice did not depend on vocabulary size (32). Combined, these results show us that retrieval practice is helpful for a wide variety of learners, from elementary to college students, regardless of vocabulary size.

Younger students have poor test-taking strategies in general and need to be coached on effective test-taking strategies. Poor test-taking strategies contribute to test anxiety and poor motivation (33). Providing additional help and coaching with test-taking strategies can help reduce test anxiety in younger students (34).

---

5. Myth: Testing causes undue anxiety and distress that is harmful to students

RESEARCH: Frequent testing actually reduces anxiety.

This might be one of the biggest criticisms of tests. A big concern of parents and teachers is that tests cause actual psychological harm to students. However, when used properly, tests can improve anxiety (35, 36). Of course, "when used properly" is a big caveat. When students are given multiple, low-stakes, retrieval practice attempts learning is improved and their anxiety is reduced.

Whether the process of retrieval comes in the form of short quizzes, group discussions, practice tests, or quiz games, students' learning will improve. Retrieval strengthens the association between cues and targets (e.g. "hello" and "hola"), provides feedback to students to let them know what information they still need to practice, and provides feedback to the instructor so he or she can guide the student (37). Furthermore, as a result of this retrieval practice, students become more confident and less anxious about tests (36). Retrieval practice does not have to be graded. Researchers found that students who were given ungraded pop-quizzes performed better on the final exam, were less anxious, and found quizzes more helpful than students who took graded pop-quizzes or no quizzes (38). In contrast, when students are given only a few high-stakes tests they miss out on the benefits of retrieval practice, including the confidence and peace of mind that comes from practice.

Research on test anxiety has found that students with poorer study skills, who are less prepared for tests, are more anxious about tests (39). In addition, the findings above show that regular, low-stakes quizzing improves test preparedness and reduces anxiety (36, 38). Taken together this suggests that it's not the test, but the lack of test preparation that causes test anxiety.

Summary
- Tests can be powerful tools to improve learning.
- Pre-tests and small quizzes leading up to bigger tests can be useful because they can help students identify what they need to study.
- Retrieval can help students see if they have been overconfident in their abilities.
- Retrieval can help students organize their knowledge, giving them a structure or system to help with future learning.
- Retrieval is most effective when it is spaced out and done multiple times.

The Tools

Retrieval practice is best used to reinforce and solidify learning. It is most effective when it's done repeatedly and over spaced intervals.

While testing is a form of retrieval practice, retrieval practice does not have to be formal assessments. Any activity that uses retrieval practice can be easily modified to fit the guidelines for quick quizzing. Classroom activities that are structured like trivia games, like Around the World and A Ticket Out the Door, use retrieval, and with a bit of tweaking can be made even more effective.

Early Elementary

- **Hints:** Younger children may need more help with some of the quiz games suggested in this section. Make sure that any activity you do with younger children is structured so that they can get hints and clues about the answers to help them out, especially if it is a new game or if you are covering new material.
- **Kaboom:** In Kaboom students draw a popsicle stick at random from a cup. Each popsicle stick has a bit of trivia on it—a vocabulary word, a math problem, a true/false statement, etc.—and they have to give the correct response to that bit of trivia in order to keep the popsicle stick. Each student takes a turn drawing sticks and answering questions until they get a stick that says KABOOM! on it. If a student draws a Kaboom stick then they have to put all of their popsicle sticks back in the cup. The game continues for as long as you want. Whenever it's time to stop, whoever has the most sticks wins! Games like this are excellent opportunities for retrieval practice because they can be done repeatedly with the same set of material. If they're played frequently then they will be taking advantage of spacing and repetition—all great things for boosting learning!
- **A Ticket Out the Door (Exit question/review):** This can be used before the end of the day, before recess, or prior to going to lunch. The teacher stands in the doorway with a set of flashcards. In order to get out of the classroom the student needs to answer one question correctly. If not, they go to the back of the line and start over.
- **Around the World:** This method of instruction and reinforcement can be used in multiple subject areas. Ask one student to stand next to another student. The instructor will ask the students a question aloud or will display a flash card, related to a topic of study, and will ask both students to determine the answer. The first student who correctly answers the question will move on to stand close to the next student. This method of instruction will allow the instructor to determine what knowledge the students have gained, where the students are struggling, and allows the students to utilize information that they have gained in the classroom. With younger students, the instructor should provide appropriate time and assistance where needed. With repeated use, the method will increase spacing and repetition for the students.

- **3–2-1 Activity:** At the end of the lesson, teachers will provide students with the 3-2-1 Activity Chart. Individual students will determine three concepts or key ideas that they have learned throughout the lesson, two important details that they remember from the lesson, and one question that they still have about the material. With younger students, instructors should provide guidance and time where needed.

Late Elementary

- **Hints:** Younger children may need more help with some of the quiz games suggested in this section. Make sure that any activity you do with younger children is structured so that they can get hints and clues about the answers to help them out, especially if it is new game or if you are covering new material.
- **Kaboom:** See above.
- **Around the World:** See above.
- **3–2-1 Activity:** See above.
- **A Ticket Out the Door (Exit question/review):** See above. As students get better at the material, you can increase the difficulty of the questions or have them answer three questions correctly before being able to leave the line.

Middle School

- **A Ticket Out the Door:** See above.
- **Kaboom:** See above.
- **Flashcards:** As students are encouraged to work more independently and study for class on their own, explaining how to use flashcards can help them get more out of their study sessions. Explain that what makes the flashcards helpful is using their memory. Encourage them to avoid "cheating." If they have to turn the flashcard over to read the answer in order to get it correct, then they really did not answer it correctly. Also explain that the more they use their memory for something, the longer they will be able to remember it. So shuffling their flashcards and going through the deck multiple times helps them learn more than just going through the deck once.

High School and College

- **Kaboom:** See above.
- **Flashcards:** See above.
- **Quick Quizzes:** In addition to the games and activities above, you can structure more frequent quizzes in your classes. Frequent quizzes not only help the students learn by improving their long-term

memory, but also give important feedback for the teacher. Students also report being more likely to complete all of their homework when more frequent quizzes are used (40). There are a number of different ways you can add quizzes to your classes and you can decide how much they should count as part of the grade, or if they should count at all. The following are a few examples of how small quizzes can be added to class.

- *VIF (Very Important Fact):* At the end of the class have students quickly write what they feel the most important thing was they learned in that lesson.
- *Homework Quiz:* Start off the class with two or three questions related to the homework or assigned reading for that day. By making students frequently accountable for homework it is more likely that they will come to class prepared. It also signals to the students what concepts will be important to pay attention to in class that day.
- *Two-Minute Quiz:* At any point during the class—in the first five minutes, when they start to glaze over, or at the very end—you can ask them to take a quick two-minute quiz. They have two minutes to write their response to two questions on the material you are going over that day.

● ● ● ● ●

References

1. Anderson JR & Schooler LJ (1991) Reflections of the environment in memory. *Psychological Science* 2(6):396–408.
2. Raaijmakers JGW & Shiffrin RM (1981) Search of associative memory. *Psychological Review* 88:93–134.
3. Szpunar KK & McDermott KB (2008) Episodic future thought and its relation to remembering: Evidence from ratings of subjective experience. *Consciousness and Cognition* 17(1):330–334.
4. Karpicke JD, Lehman M, & Aue WR (2014) Retrieval-based learning: An episodic context account. *Psychology of Learning and Motivation*, ed. Ross BH (Elsevier Academic Press, San Diego, CA), Vol 61.
5. Whitten WB & Bjork RA (1977) Learning from tests: The effects of spacing. *Journal of Verbal Learning and Verbal Behavior* 16:465–478.
6. Roediger HL, McDermott KB, & McDaniel MA (2011) Using testing to improve learning and memory. *Psychology and the real world: Essays illustrating fundamental contributions to society*, ed. Gernsbacher MA, Pew RW, Hough L, & Pomerantz JR (Worth Publishing Co, New York), pp 65–74.
7. Tulving E (1974) Cue-dependent forgetting. *American Scientist* 62(1):74–82.
8. Karpicke JD & Bauernschmidt A (2011) Spaced retrieval: Absolute spacing enhances learning regardless of relative spacing. *Journal of Experimental Psychology: Learning, Memory, Cognition* 37(5):1250–1257.

9. Benjamin AS & Tullis J (2010) What makes distributed practice effective? *Cognitive Psychology* 61:228–247.
10. Karpicke JD, Blunt JR, & Smith MA (2016) Retrieval-based learning: Positive effects of retrieval practice in elementary school children. *Frontiers in Psychology* 7.
11. Smith MA & Karpicke JD (2014) Retrieval practice with short-answer, multiple-choice, and hybrid tests. *Memory* 22(7):784–802.
12. Agarwal PK, Bain PM, & Chamberlain RW (2012) The value of applied research: Retrieval practice improves classroom learning and recommendations from a teacher, a principal, and a scientist. *Educational Psychology Review* 24:437–448.
13. Roediger HL & Karpicke JD (2006) Test-enhanced learning. *Psychological Science* 17(3):249–255.
14. Greene RL (2008) Repetition and spacing effects. *Learning and memory: A comprehensive reference*, ed. Roediger HL (Elsevier, Oxford, England), pp 65–78.
15. Karpicke JD & Roediger HL (2007) Repeated retrieval during learning is the key to long-term retention. *Journal of Memory and Language* 57:151–162.
16. Rohrer D (2012) Interleaving helps students distinguish among similar concepts. *Educational Psychology Review* 24:355–367.
17. Kang SH & Pashler H (2012) Learning painting styles: Spacing is advantageous when it promotes discriminative contrast. *Applied Cognitive Psychology* 26(1):97–103.
18. Taylor K & Rohrer D (2016) The effects of interleaved practice. *Applied Cognitive Psychology* 24:837–848.
19. Amlund JT, Kardash CAM, & Kulhavy RM (1986) Repetitive reading and recall of expository text. *Reading Research Quarterly* 21:49–58.
20. Izawa C (1966) Reinforcement-test sequences in paired-associate learning. *Psychological Reports* 18:879–919.
21. Arnold KM & McDermott KB (2010) Test-potentiated learning: Distinguishing between direct and indirect effects of tests. *Journal of Experimental Psychology: Learning, Memory, Cognition* 39(3):90–95.
22. Zaromb FL & Roediger HL (2010) The testing effect in free recall is associated with enhanced organizational processes. *Memory & Cognition* 38(8):955–1008.
23. Karpicke JD & Grimaldi PJ (2012) Retrieval-based learning: A perspective for enhancing meaningful learning. *Educational Psychology Review* 24(3):401–418.
24. Jacoby LL, Wahlheim CN, & Coane JH (2010) Test-enhanced learning of natural concepts: Effects of recognition memory, classification, and metacognition. *Journal of Experimental Psychology: Learning, Memory, Cognition* 36:1441–1451.
25. Butler AC (2010) Repeated testing produces superior transfer of learning relative to repeated studying. *Journal of Experimental Psychology: Learning, Memory, Cognition* 36:1118–1133.
26. McDaniel MA, Thomas RC, Agarwal PK, McDermott KB, & Roediger HL (2013) Quizzing in middle-school science: Successful transfer performance on classroom exams. *Applied Cognitive Psychology* 27:360–372.
27. Leeming JK (2002) The exam-a-day procedure improves performance in psychology classes. *Teaching of Psychology* 29(3):210–212.
28. Trumbo MC, Leiting KA, McDaniel MA, & Hodge GK (2016) Effects of reinforcement on test-enhanced learning in a large, diverse introductory college psychology course. *Journal of Experimental Psychology: Applied* 22(2):148–160.

29. Black P & Wilam D (1998) Assessment and classroom learning. *Assessment in Education: Principles, Policy & Best Practice* 5:7–74.
30. Fritz CO, Morris PE, Nolan D, & Singleton J (2007) Expanding retrieval practice: An effective aid to preschool children's learning. *Quarterly Journal of Experimental Psychology* 60:991–1004.
31. Goossens NAM, Camp G, Verkoeijen PPJL, & Tabbers HK (2014) The effect of retrieval practice in primary school vocabulary learning. *Applied Cognitive Psychology* 28:135–142.
32. Goossens NAM, Camp G, Verkoeijen PPJL, Tabbers HK, & Zwann RA (2014) The benefit of retrieval practice over elaborative restudy in primary school vocabulary learning. *Journal of Applied Research: Memory & Cognition* 3:177–182.
33. Dodeen HM, Abdelfattah F, & Alshumrani S (2014) Test-taking skills of secondary students: The relationship with motivation, attitudes, anxiety and attitudes towards tests. *South African Journal of Education* 34(2):1–18.
34. Ergene T (2003) Effective interventions on test anxiety reduction. *School Psychology International* 24(3):313–328.
35. Benjamin AS & McDermott KB (2015) The value of standardized testing: A perspective from cognitive psychology. *Policy Insights from the Behavioral and Brain Sciences* 2:13–23.
36. Agarwal PK, D'Antonio L, Roediger HL, III, McDermott KB, & McDaniel MA (2014) Classroom-based programs of retrieval practice reduce middle school and high school students' test anxiety. *Journal of Applied Research in Memory and Cognition* 3:131–139.
37. Roediger HL, Putnam AL, & Smith MA (2011) Ten benefits of testing and their applications to educational practice. *Psychology of learning and motivation: Cognition in education*, ed. Ross JMB (Elsevier, Oxford, England), pp 1–36.
38. Khanna MM (2015) Ungraded pop-quizzes: Test-enhanced learning without all the anxiety. *Teaching of Psychology* 42(2):174–178.
39. Numan A & Hasan SS (2017) Effect of study habits on test anxiety and academic achievement of undergraduate students. *Journal of Research and Reflections in Education* 11(1):1–14.
40. Lyle KB & Crawford NA (2011) Retrieving essential material at the end of lectures improves performance on statistics exams. *Teaching of Psychology* 38:94–97.

5

Learning Styles

Learning styles refers to the idea that people have inborn styles of learning that predispose them to enhanced learning if information is presented in their style. Specifically, it encompasses a set of theories that promote the idea that students learn better when material is presented in their preferred mode; i.e. visually, verbally, kinesthetically, etc. This chapter reveals that, contrary to popular belief, we all learn in fundamentally very similar ways and discusses how teachers can use the concept of dual coding to help all students learn.

The Myths

1. Every person has their own learning style, some are visual learners, some are kinesthetic, some linguistic, etc.
2. Teaching in the student's preferred learning style makes a difference in how well the student will learn the information.
3. It is good practice to identify students' learning styles and create lesson plans to address those learning styles.
4. There is no danger in teaching to students' preferred learning styles.

The Research

The basic idea behind learning styles is that if the teacher matches the delivery mode of instruction to the student's preferred learning style then learning is enhanced. This idea, called the **matching hypothesis**, forms the basis for learning styles as an instructional model. This model has received international acceptance in both the public and academic arenas because learning styles seem to be a self-evident component of who we are as individuals.

The concept of learning styles has repeatedly been called a **neuromyth**—a misunderstanding of how the brain functions—by cognitive scientists and neuroscientists alike. Instead, research strongly supports the dual coding theory. For more than 20 years educational and cognitive psychologists have known that learning information in two ways, visually and verbally, improves memory. In a review of the literature Mayer (1) reported that **dual coding**, using pictures side by side with text, is the best way to present novel material to learners. Pairing visual and verbal forms of the material increased learning outcomes across the board, especially when learning new information.

In an excellent review article titled "Dual coding theory and education," Paivio (2) explains that "cognition is the variable pattern of interplay of the two systems" (p. 230). He relays that verbal and nonverbal memories can have an additive effect on recall, saying that if you code a memory with both verbal and image **cues**, information is more likely to be found in long-term memory. Because the visual and linguistic information has separate pathways, the visual information will not interfere with the learning of the verbal information, rather it helps tag the information, giving the information more cues, more connections, leading to better memory of the information. The bare bones message is that from grade school to the university, across all subject areas, when instructors pair text with images (or imagery) memory and recall is enhanced (2).

Connections

Dual coding is effective because it provides more cues to help memory. In Chapter 4: Testing we discussed how memory is cue-dependent. In that chapter we reviewed how to use retrieval practice to make cues more powerful, making it easier for you to remember target information. Part of the reason why dual coding is effective is because it provides multiple cues for memory. This makes it easier for students to build connections between ideas and remember them in different contexts.

Unlike learning styles, which focuses on tailoring lessons to certain students, dual coding is beneficial for all learners. Findings from a meta-analysis published in *Educational Psychology Review* indicated that not only do learners remember better when pairing images with text, but to further help those with poor spatial ability, dynamic visualization (like animation or interactive images) and 3D images work better for memory than pictures (3). This informs us that not only does pairing verbal material with images improve learning, but further, if the images are 3D or dynamic, then dual coding helps those with poor spatial ability.

> **Development**
>
> According to dual coding theory, those with poorer vocabularies, like young children, who lack verbal cues to an image, are less likely to remember the image than an adult (someone with language to name or describe the image). This informs us of how important language and vocabulary are for memory, especially for children (2).
>
> Children of all ages remember words better when helped with pictures than pictures when helped with words. This was not the case in adults, which gives us a key element of developmental learning: adults, those with large vocabularies, have an advantage over individuals with small vocabularies. The reason is that with a larger vocabulary you have more tags or cues to attach to images and information (2).

Now that we have introduced the evidence-based theory of dual coding, we will return to the myths and research on learning styles. Our introduction of dual coding should help integrate and shed light on the research that debunks learning styles theory.

1. Myth: Every person has their own learning style, some are visual learners, some are kinesthetic, some linguistic, etc.

>   ***RESEARCH:*** *While we all differ in many ways—our likes, dislikes, motivation, past experience, our developmental environment, our range of abilities, etc.—we all learn in fundamentally similar ways.*

Belief in learning styles is staggering. It is widespread among school teachers (4) and higher education fares no better; in a study looking at faculty in the U.S., 64 percent agreed that learning is enhanced if the instruction is matched to students' learning styles (5). Despite the widespread belief in learning styles, there is very little empirical evidence to support it. In 2008 a group of cognitive psychologists attempted to write a review of experimental evidence for learning styles. To their dismay, they not only found a lack of experiments that support learning styles, but a lack of experiments on learning styles at all (6). They therefore outlined the criteria for demonstrating learning styles empirically. Following this pivotal paper many other researchers published papers reporting this lack of empirical evidence for the learning styles model (7–14).

For teachers the issue is quite confusing, seeing papers published in professional journals that report results supporting either the learning styles model or the matching hypothesis or both. A key aspect of learning styles is the matching hypothesis; the idea that teaching to a student's preferred learning style will improve his or her learning, that learning styles are causal to learning. To demonstrate that this is true an experiment must show that conditions where learning style and instruction are matched perform better than conditions where learning style and instruction are not matched. Such an experiment would have to randomly assign students to one of at least two different learning methods (e.g. visual or kinesthetic) and give all students the same final test so that they can be directly compared. These three criteria: random assignment to different learning methods, the same final test, and, most crucially, demonstration that students who were taught in a learning method that matched their learning style performed best on the final test must be met in order to show that learning style affects learning. Pashler *et al.* (6) systematically scoured the academic literature and listed a large set of published studies whose designs were simply unable to identify causal effects, a benefit of learning styles, or to even test the matching hypothesis yet they still reported support for the learning styles model!

This, fellow classroom teachers, reveals a big problem with interpretation of credible research.

Despite the empirical evidence repeatedly showing no support for learning styles, teacher educators, teacher education programs, and best practices have endorsed this model to help differentiate instruction, and show parents and the general public that teachers are being trained to help every child learn. This lack of empirical support also did not stop teacher educators or general teacher education textbooks (see Cuevas, 2016 (7)) from supporting, and advocating that the next generation of teachers base their lesson planning and teaching on students' learning styles. What makes this even more frustrating is that there is a multitude of published research seemingly supporting the learning styles model. General education textbooks both promote learning styles and fail to address the fact that there is a lack of empirical support. In an article by An & Car (15), entitled "Learning styles theory fails to explain learning and achievement" the authors strike at the heart of this myth, stating "most important, learning styles theorists have ignored the research that directly contradicts learning style theories" (p. 2). Sadly, it is no wonder that the learning styles model continues to proliferate in classrooms internationally from pre-K to college graduate programs. Learning styles may be the biggest hoax played on teachers and educators in the past 50 years.

2. Myth: Teaching in the student's preferred learning style makes a difference in how well the student will learn the information

> **RESEARCH:** *A multitude of empirical studies have shown that teaching to students' preferred learning style makes absolutely no difference in performance outcomes.*

Even if the concept of learning styles wasn't conceptually flawed, even if we had evidence that individuals displayed this neuromyth called learning styles, would you alter your lesson plans, would you spend your valuable time and limited resources on efforts to match your teaching to your students' learning styles if you knew it made no difference in learning outcomes?

As of 2017 there has not been a single published study that shows evidence that tailor-made learning styles lesson plans improve a student's achievement (15, 16). Not only is there no evidence that catering to learning styles helps students, there is good reason to think that it may be holding them back. By tailoring lesson plans to learning styles, presenting material only in students' preferred mode, we are ignoring weaknesses that can be strengthened. Rather than matching instruction to students' learning styles, educators are much better served by connecting new information with existing knowledge and adding sensory (most important are visual and verbal) cues to the new information. An and Carr (15) specifically indicate that visual and verbal thinking can be improved over time.

A simple example of how you can use both visual and verbal information, dual coding, to help all students comes from a clever experiment using presentation slides, similar to PowerPoint. Issa *et al.* (17) compared the memory of students given traditional, bullet-point-heavy slides, to a group of students that received slides that only presented key words with pictures, and the pictures were explained verbally. In-text concepts and definitions were left off of the slides. Results indicated superior memory and retention of information in the key words and pictures group compared to the bullet-point-heavy group. This study has very practical information for all of those teachers and professors who use PowerPoint or similar software. Learning is enhanced when PowerPoint is used as a visual tag that later is used as a cue to help locate the information in long-term memory. However, note that learning is harmed if students are trying to write down verbal bullet points while simultaneously trying to listen to and understand what the educator is saying.

Connections

Presentation tools like PowerPoint can be excellent at improving learning through the use of dual coding. They make it easy to present verbal and visual information together, which helps give students more cues to improve their understanding and memory of the material. However, if they are rushed through without giving students time to process the

> visual and verbal information, you may be inadvertently forcing students to multitask. In Chapter 1: Multitasking we talked about how multitasking actually hurts attention and memory by forcing students to switch between multiple tasks. Give students time to take notes from the slides before talking about them or elaborating to avoid having to multitask.

So how did we get here? Why do so many books and teaching guides recommend tailoring instruction to different learning styles when there is no credible evidence that doing so helps students? Because learning is personal. Because we are so close to it that it is difficult to evaluate.

> Basic research on human learning and memory, especially research on human metacognition ... has demonstrated that our intuitions and beliefs about how we learn are often wrong in serious ways. We do not ... gain an understanding of the complexities of human learning and memory from the trials and errors of everyday living and learning. ... [P]eople hold beliefs about how they learn that are faulty ... which frequently leads people to ... teach in nonoptimal ways.
> (Pashler et al., 2008, p. 117 (6))

We used this quote in the introduction to highlight how difficult it is to study learning in general, but the authors were referring specifically to learning styles. These deeply held beliefs about learning styles and lack of objective studies have led to several breakdowns in the research and reporting system:

1. Authors of research that fails to incorporate a methodological design capable of testing whether teaching to a preferred learning style results in improved outcomes, still report positive results.
2. Journal editors failed to identify this, or stop the articles from being published.
3. Authors of research *who did* use a methodological design that is able to establish that teaching to a student's learning style improves learning outcomes, found no evidence, but nevertheless reported findings in favor of learning styles.
4. Journal editors failed to identify this, or stop the articles from being published.
5. Professors and other educators with training in research methodology, failed to pick up on either design flaws in the research, or reporting flaws in the research.

6. Last, general education textbooks also fail to identify this glaring problem of a well-accepted theory having no empirical support.

This is a major flaw (or several major flaws) in the system that has been created to produce a flow of information to teachers and the public!

3. Myth: It is good practice to identify students' learning styles and create lesson plans to address those learning styles

RESEARCH: There is a serious lack of validity and reliability in learning styles inventories, and focusing on learning styles wastes time and money on lesson planning and purchasing the instruments.

One of the most damning pieces of evidence against learning styles is that the learning style inventories that are supposed to accurately measure and categorize students into different learning style categories (i.e. visual, verbal, etc.) are not valid. In Chapter 4: Testing we talked about test **validity**—the extent to which a test accurately measures what it is supposed to measure. For more than 30 years we have known that many of the learning styles inventories have, at best, questionable validity and reliability (18). Added to this problem is the fact that most measurement tools of learning styles are self-report inventories which add a host of other credibility concerns.

Another issue with learning styles inventories is that they are not reliable. Test **reliability** refers to whether the results of a test are consistent each time a student takes a test. Does it make sense that a student could be a visual learner on Monday, an auditory learner on Thursday, and a kinesthetic learner on the weekend? Most learning styles measurement tools are not reliable (15, 19). The issue is not just with new tests. An and Carr (15) report that "Neither the original Learning Style Inventory (Kolb, 1976) nor revised Learning Style Inventory (Kolb, 1985) has good test-retest reliability" (p. 2). This lack of reliability, leading students to score differently on the same learning styles test at different points in time, is part of what makes learning styles tests not valid. How can they accurately measure what they are supposed to measure if they can't reliably measure it in the first place? Even if learning styles inventories were accurately measuring learning styles and it just so happened that learning styles changed over time, this lack of reliability makes it even more frustrating to tailor lesson plans to learning styles.

Without credible evidence on which to base administering learning style instruments to students, teachers, administrators, professors and the like can better allocate their time and resources to evidence-based methods of improving learning. Further, as educators it is our responsibility to seek out ways to help students in the areas where their skill set is lacking, rather than transforming our instruction to cater to a non-existing learning style.

4. Myth: There is no danger in teaching to students' preferred learning styles

> *RESEARCH: There are a plethora of reasons why NOT to engage in a theory that does not have evidence to support it, most notably that the theory is conceptually flawed.*

There are a number of reasons why using learning styles can be harmful. One of the more important is that students get "pigeon holed" into particular styles, influencing their confidence, perceived abilities, and self-efficacy (4). Another unfortunate effect of failing to debunk learning styles, noted by Newman and Miah (4), is that the public is now aware of this concept and often criticize teachers for failing to teach to a student's particular learning style: "learning styles theories, when invoked, are most often offered as an explanation for poor classroom performance" (p. 268). In other words, if educators continue to use learning styles then teachers will continue to be criticized for failing to properly use a theory that doesn't work to begin with.

There are, of course, many other reasons why continuing to use learning styles can be harmful. These include: wasting valuable time, money, and other resources on an ineffective model; the unwarranted expectations of students, teachers, and parents; and eroding or damaging the very foundation of the trust that the public has in our educational institutions. This last point is not to be taken lightly. Without trust from the public as to educators' knowledge of what works and what doesn't work to influence learning in children, the system will not have buy in, and will fail.

A good theory needs to explain the cognitive or neurological reasons *why* people supposedly have different learning styles, not just describe preferences. It should also outline the developmental implications, for example what developmental environments detract or enhance certain learning styles and what genetic or biological prerequisites are necessary for a visual learner. This lack of solid explanatory framework adds to the list of reasons why learning styles is conceptually flawed (15). However, one thing that evidence on learning styles does inform us about is that individuals believe that they have preferences for learning. There is good evidence that students express strong and consistent preferences (20). Despite these preferences there is no evidence that if a student prefers to receive visual instead of verbal information that they actually benefit from such instruction. Our intuitions about our learning are often wrong and we are poor at predicting what conditions are best for our learning (21).

Given what we have outlined in this chapter, teacher educators need to review the relevant empirical evidence, and make much needed changes at the collegiate level, including choice of textbooks, and begin to make choices in teaching and learning that are well supported by rigorous research. Educational leaders in the field, political affiliates, and those third parties who help bring research to teachers are all needed to dispel this strongly held myth. Terms like "evidence-based teaching," "data-driven instruction," and the like, must reflect the current state of credible research, instead of myth-based educational rhetoric.

Summary

- From the elementary grades to the university, across all subject areas, when instructors pair text with images (or imagery) memory and recall is enhanced.
- This dual coding is well supported by decades of research in the scientific literature.
- Learning styles is a neuromyth.
- Despite the popularity of learning styles, repeated reviews of the scientific literature reveal that there is **no** empirical evidence that learning styles exist.
- Most studies that support learning styles do not use a research design that that would even allow for the testing of the matching hypothesis.
- Not a single piece of evidence shows that learning is enhanced by tailoring lessons to match students' learning styles.
- Learning style inventories are not reliable or valid.
- Use of learning styles models to frame curriculum harms students, teachers, parents, administration, and generally the field of education.

● ● ● ● ●

The Tools

People tend to learn in the same way. While there are some individual differences, the same basic processes occur across individuals. There is no such thing as a "visual" or an "auditory" learner. Developing activities or complex lesson plans catering to certain styles of learning is simply a waste of time. However, getting information in different ways can be beneficial. Dual coding and **multimodal** presentations help learning for all learners. Students tend to have better recognition and recall of information that has been presented linguistically with a visual tag that conceptually connects with the language. Activities/guidelines should be things that are beneficial for everyone in the classroom (not just a "visual" or an "auditory" learner).

Early Elementary

- **Around the Room:** Students use material around the room and insights from other students to answer questions. Questions can be derived from any subject. Students can socialize with other students to answer questions so it utilizes social skills as well as problem-solving skills.
- **Act the Word:** Assign students to groups of three or four students. Give content words to each group and have group members learn the meaning of each word. Then, instruct group members to come up with different ways to act out each word and teach to the class. The rest of the class is then taught how to act out the words and the group members tell them the meaning and how to pronounce it. After all the groups have taught their action, have the class stand in a circle and call out a word for the students to act out, say the meaning, and the word. Students should explain their performances and how the activity improved their understanding of the word. This activity helps the students develop an understanding of content vocabulary and material. With younger grades, assistance and guidance should be provided when needed.

Late Elementary

- **Act the Word:** See above.
- **Visual Enhancements:** When imagery and other forms of visual representation are included in classroom examples, it strengthens the impact of the material. This allows students to engage with the material on multiple levels and develop different lines of thinking and questioning to further the learning process.
- **Scavenger Hunts:** This technique requires the use and development of a wide variety of skills. Through the utilization of socialization, communication, deduction, and problem-solving skills, students will interact with other students, teachers, and community members to solve puzzles and complete tasks.
- **Around the Room:** See above.

Middle School

- **Self-made:** Students develop questions and ask them of their classmates, effectively quizzing themselves and their classmates by developing and answering questions based on the material.
- **Guided Note:** Guided notes are a great technique for establishing many different connections to the learned material. This technique provides an outline of the material to be learned and allows students to fill in the spaces with helpful and memorable parts of the lecture.
- **Visual Representation:** The instructor will assign a selected reading to the students. The students will then be instructed to compare and contrast an excerpt from the text with a cultural artifact. The students will explain the connection the visual representation has to the reading selection and will explain how the visual representation and the reading selection differ. This activity assists students in synthesizing new information in an alternative and meaningful way.

High School and College

- **Self-made:** See above.
- **Visual Representation:** See above.
- **Presentations:** Student-made presentations are often very helpful in disseminating information to their peers. Having a new voice present the information in a novel way can help create fun and creative ways for remembering material.

References

1. Mayer RE (1997) Multimedia learning: Are we asking the right questions? *Educational Psychologist* 32(1):1–19.
2. Paivio A (2006) Dual coding theory and education. Draft chapter presented at the conference on Pathways to Literacy Achievement for High Poverty Children at the University of Michigan School of Education.
3. Hoffler TN (2010) Spatial ability: Its influence on learning with visualizations—a meta-analytic review. *Educational Psychology Review* 22:245–269.
4. Newman PM & Miah M (2017) Evidence-based higher education—is the learning styles "myth" important? *Frontiers in Psychology* 8.
5. Dandy K & Bendersky K (2014) Student and faculty beliefs about learning in higher education: Implications for teaching. *International Journal of Teaching and Learning in Higher Education* 26:258–380.
6. Pashler H, McDaniel MA, Roher D, & Bjork RA (2008) Learning styles: Concepts and evidence. *Psychological Science in the Public Interest* 9(3):105–119.
7. Cuevas J (2016) An analysis of current evidence supporting two alternate learning models: Learning styles and dual coding. *Journal of Educational Sciences and Psychology* 6(1):1–13.

8. Allcock SJ & Hulme JA (2010) Learning styles in the classroom: Educational benefit or planning exercise? *Psychology Teaching Review* 16(2):67–79.
9. Bishka A (2010) Learning styles fray: Brilliant or batty? *Performance Improvement* 49(10):9–13.
10. Mayer RE (2011) Does styles research have useful implications for educational practice? *Learning & Individual Differences* 21(3):319–320.
11. Norman G (2009) When will learning style go out of style? *Advances in Health Sciences Education* 14(1):1–4.
12. Riener C & Willingham DT (2010) The myth of learning styles. *Change* 42(5):32–35.
13. Rohrer D & Pashler H (2012) Learning styles: Where's the evidence? *Medical Education* 46(7):634–635.
14. Scott C (2010) The enduring appeal of "learning styles". *Australian Journal of Education* 54(1):5–17.
15. An D & Carr M (2017) Learning styles theory fails to explain learning and achievement: Recommendations for alternative approaches. *Personality and Individual Differences* 116: 410-416.
16. Bretz SL (2017) Finding no evidence for learning styles. *Journal of Chemical Education* 94(7):825–826.
17. Issa N, Schuller M, Santacaterina S, *et al.* (2011) Applying multimedia design principles enhances learning in medical education. *Medical Education* 45(8):818–826.
18. Platsidou M & Metallidou P (2009) Validity and reliability issues of two learning style inventories in a Greek sample: Kolb's learning style inventory and Felder & Soloman's index of learning styles. *International Journal of Teaching and Learning in Higher Education* 20:324–335.
19. Willingham DT, Hughes EM, & Dobolyi DG (2015) The scientific status of learning styles theories. *Teaching of Psychology* 42(3):266–271.
20. Massa LJ & Mayer RE (2006) Testing the ATI hypothesis: Should multimedia instruction accommodate verbalizer-visualizer cognitive style? *Learning and Individual Differences* 16:321–335.
21. Schmidt RA & Bjork RA (1992) New conceptualizations of practice: Common principles in three paradigms suggest new concepts for training. *Psychological Science* 3(4):207–217.

Afterword •••••

Technology in the Classroom

A common theme that has crept up through several of these chapters has been the use, and misuse, of technology. For example, both multitasking and selective attention highlight how easily technology distracts students from learning. Often, technology like cell phones, TVs, and laptops leads to distracting environments for students. However, we have also given examples of how technology can be used as a tool to improve learning. Tools like online flashcards and quiz games help students review material by using retrieval practice and presentation tools and interactive websites help students learn through dual coding. In this section we will reconcile these two different points of view and emphasize how to use technology in the classroom instead of letting it use you.

First of all, it is worth pointing out that technology in the classroom is not a new phenomenon. As far back as Plato, people have been bemoaning technological advances in the classroom. Plato was famously against writing and felt that teaching students to write encouraged laziness and forgetfulness. In somewhat more modern times, using an overhead instead of a chalkboard was a technological advancement. Even more recently, using a PowerPoint instead of an overhead was a technologically adept maneuver. The conversation surrounding technology in the classroom is not new. In all of these cases, while there was initial concern that the mode of presentation would affect the quality of the learning, people eventually saw them as simply tools of the trade. Second, technology is a broad term that can refer to anything from overhead projectors to smart boards, from Google to Twitter, or from a typewriter to a tablet. All of these technologies can help or hurt learning to various degrees. As educators it is our job to decide what works best in our classrooms. Any amount of guilt over using or not using these technologies should be put away immediately. If you have an awesome activity that involves pen and paper that helps out in your lesson, use it. Don't worry about not being on top of the trends. If you have an engaging class project that involves campaigning with twitter hashtags, great! Keep doing that.

Technology in and of itself is not good or bad. It's not going to save us all, and it's not going to cause the downfall of civilization as we know it. Adding technology to your classroom isn't going to turn it into an overnight success. Going without the latest classroom gadgets doesn't make you irrelevant or out of touch. The key to using, or not using, technology in the classroom is a basic understanding of how it affects students' attention and learning.

In Chapter 1: Multitasking, we debunked the myth that multitasking is a useful skill that allows us to work on several tasks at once. Instead, multitasking involves switching your attention between multiple tasks at a high cost to memory and learning. Having the TV on in the background while studying, reading text messages while listening to a lecture, reading through presentation slides while listening to a lecture, and taking notes on a laptop are all examples of technology enabling multitasking. Students perform better on tasks and remember more of the presented material when they are single-tasking. Doing homework and then watching TV, turning cell phones off while in classes or meetings, giving students time to read slides before discussing them, and taking notes on paper are all ways to get around the detrimental effects of multitasking with technology.

In Chapter 2: Examples, we explained why multiple examples are better than one and how students use examples to learn and become interested. While examples can potentially make a topic more interesting, it's important to be aware of what kind of interest you are generating and how seductive details can trick students into remembering the wrong information. Social media and the internet can be a powerful tool to connect students with different examples and resources to help them engage with a topic. A common pitfall, however, is that without the skills to assess these sources of information students can end up relying on sources that are not credible. In addition, without much experience with the topic students can still be susceptible to seductive details of examples and rely on surface features instead of extracting the more important structural details.

In Chapter 3: Focus, we explained how focused attention is a skill that can be learned. Somewhat counterintuitively, focus can be improved by *adding* distractions instead of taking them away. By learning to ignore irrelevant stimuli, we learn to set attentional priorities and focus on what is important. Notifications on cell phones and computers are designed to grab our attention and have trained us to pay attention to them. Learning how to manage these notifications and ignore these pieces of technological distraction can help students focus on learning.

In Chapter 4: Testing, we debunked the myth that tests hurt learning and discussed the research on retrieval practice. Retrieval is the process of rebuilding a memory in order to call information to mind. Every time something is recalled and a student goes through the process of retrieval, they get better at rebuilding the memory, making it easier to remember the information in the future.

In Chapter 5: Learning Styles, we debunked the myth that every person has their own learning style and catering to that learning style improves learning. There is no such thing as a "visual" or "verbal" learner. However, presenting information both visually and verbally helps all learners. Technology in the classroom can definitely help with dual coding—receiving information visually and verbally. Websites, blogs, and news articles can all be excellent resources for examples of visual and verbal materials.

●●●●●

Technologies in the Classroom

Here is a short review of a handful of technologies used in the classroom. We will discuss each in terms of how they can potentially help and hurt learning so that you can evaluate them for yourself to see how to use (or not use!) them in the classroom.

Presentation Tools

Presentation tools like PowerPoint are an older technology so it may seem a bit weird to include it on this list. Just because it's a more comfortable and familiar form of technology in the classroom doesn't mean it's not worth examining. In fact, we think that makes it more important to examine because we may not be as critical of it.

How Presentation Tools Help Us

The biggest thing that presentation tools like PowerPoint, Prezi, or similar tools have going for them is their ease of use. Teachers and students alike are familiar with them and feel relatively comfortable making and sharing presentations. Teachers can easily edit and update old slides which helps keep lessons fresh and up to date. Students can and will request copies of presentation slides to help them take notes. From a learning standpoint, these tools can be especially useful in promoting dual coding since it is an easy way to present text and pictures.

How Presentation Tools Hurt Us

It can be very easy to misuse presentation tools and force students to multitask. Talking over slides while giving students time to read and then write down notes forces them to switch between reading, writing, and paying attention to you. Be mindful of what you are demanding of your students in these situations. Instead of talking through slides, give students a moment to read and process what is on the screen before launching into your explanation of it.

Online Quizzing

There are a variety of ways in which technology can help you and your students use retrieval practice—from websites devoted to making flashcards, like *Quizlet* (quizlet.com), to websites and apps that allow you to use interactive quizzes and surveys in the class like *socrative* (www.socrative.com) or *Poll Everywhere* (www.polleverywhere.com).

How Online Quizzing Helps Us

Online quizzing can be an excellent tool to help students practice retrieval. Using online quizzes and surveys in your class, like *socrative* and *Poll Everywhere* can not only be an easy way to use retrieval practice in class, they can also provide real-time feedback on student performance and perceptions, they can be used as activities instead of formal assessments, and, because you can give students the option of seeing the results, these quizzes can be interactive and engaging. However, these tools will be more effective if they can ensure that students are spacing out their retrieval and interleaving.

How Online Quizzing Hurts Us

When online quizzes are used in the classroom they can be a helpful tool for students and teachers alike. However, because students will need their laptops or phones to use these tools, introducing them into the class can invite multitasking and distraction into the lesson. Students can easily switch over to social media while taking the quizzes and it may be difficult to re-focus them back on the lesson. Be mindful of how and when you are using these tools and be aware of how students are using their devices during class.

Another pitfall to be aware of is that students may use flashcards generated by other people, and therefore these may not be appropriate flashcards for your class. By and large, these types of online quizzing tools can be very helpful in student learning.

Personal Laptops/Tablets

Personal laptops and tablets are becoming increasingly popular in the classroom. As laptops become smaller and lighter and tablets become more powerful, they are easier for students to bring to class.

How Personal Laptops/Tablets Help Us

Personal laptops and tablets have awesome computing power and capabilities. They provide students with access to a multitude of resources—from word-processing programs to the internet. When used correctly they can help students engage with material, generate new examples, apply what they have learned, and use retrieval.

How Personal Laptops/Tablets Hurt Us

Laptops and tablets in the classroom can be incredibly distracting for both the student with the device and the students around them. Having these devices out makes it easy for students to do multiple things at once—check Twitter, type notes, and listen to the teacher. In other words, laptops and tablets encourage multitasking. Even if a student doesn't use a laptop, if they see other students' screens they are easily distracted by the notifications on their screen and end up multitasking, too.

Cell Phones

Cell phones are becoming more and more pervasive in every aspect of our lives. These handy little devices rarely leave our side and are frequently found causing distractions in the classroom.

How Cell Phones Help Us

Like laptops and tablets cell phones have awesome computing power. Our mobile devices give us access to limitless information, mountains of social media, games, videos, texts, tweets, instagrams and much, much more. When used correctly they can do all the things that laptops and tablets can do: help students engage with the material, generate new examples, apply what they have learned, and use retrieval.

How Cell Phones Hurt Us

Cell phones hurt our ability to focus. They distract people when they ring, harm attention on tasks, and hurt memory. Cell phones make you multitask whether you intend to or not because they are designed to attract your attentional focus. By switching your attention between your cell phone and whatever it is that you are supposed to be doing instead, cell phones hurt attention, learning, and memory. We should be careful when allowing cell phones in class during activities and mindful of how we interact with our cell phones. These powerful devices can be powerful distractions.

* * * * *

The Conversation So Far

Learning is an exciting and challenging phenomenon to study. Despite close personal experiences with learning, we are often

Afterword

unaware of the processes at work and our own faulty assumptions about those processes. This makes it all the more important to continue to investigate and question our own theories about how we learn. This book is an attempt to start a conversation about learning with those who are closest to it: educators, students, researchers, program directors, and policy makers. We invite you to continue the conversation by contacting us at the Center for Attention, Learning, and Memory (sbucalm.blog). We hope you enjoyed this book!

Glossary

Analogical problem solving: Refers to the process by which people solve problems that are similar, or analogous, to each other.

Attention switching: A series of processes required to move attention from one task to another.

Attentional switch/task switching: Rapidly switching our focus from one task to another.

Cue-dependent: Refers to the fact that memories, specifically the retrieval of memories, are associated with and initiated by cues.

Cues: Anything that triggers a memory.

Dual coding: A well-supported theory that explains that verbal and nonverbal memories can have an additive effect on recall, stating that if you code a memory with both verbal and image cues, information is more likely to be found in long-term memory.

Individual interest: A type of interest that is an enduring characteristic of a person that causes them to respond positively towards a topic and actively seek it out.

Learning styles: Refers to the idea that people have inborn styles of learning that predispose them to enhanced learning if that information is presented in their style.

Matching hypothesis: Matching the style of the delivery mode of instruction to the student's preferred learning style enhances learning.

Media multitasking: People's ability, or skill, to use several types of technology to get many things done seemingly simultaneously.

Multimodal: Having several modes (i.e. visual or verbal) of representation.

Multitasking: People's ability, or skill, to get many things done seemingly simultaneously.

Neuromyth: A misunderstanding of how the brain functions.

Reliability: Refers to whether the results of a test are consistent each time a student takes the test.

Retrieval: The process of rebuilding a memory in order to call information to mind.

Schema: A mental framework that organizes information, allowing a person to interpret experiences and situations.

Seductive details: Details of a problem that are both interesting and irrelevant, but nonetheless tend to be remembered.

Selective attention: A person's ability/skill to attend to task-relevant stimuli and ignore task-irrelevant stimuli.

Single tasking: Performing one task at a time.

Situational interest: Temporary interest generated by the situation.

Structural details: Details of a problem that are important processes and properties that are relevant for solving the problem.

Surface details: Details of a problem that are often irrelevant for solving the problem.

Validity: The extent to which a test accurately measures what it is supposed to measure.